Cities of the New Testament

E. M. BLAIKLOCK, Litt.D.
Professor of Classics, University of Auckland New Zealand

FLEMING H. REVELL COMPANY
1965

Westwood, N.J.—316 Third Avenue
Los Angeles 41—2173 Colorado Boulevard
London, E.C.4.—29 Ludgate Hill
Glasgow, C.2.—229 Bothwell Street

Contents

Illustrations

Facing page

Introduction

CITIES dominate ancient history. The tumbled terrain of Greece saw to it that the Greek people gathered rather in compact communities than in the scattered cantonments of plainsmen. Trouble and invasion prompted the use of fortress sites with an acropolis as look-out and place of refuge. The pattern followed the Greek colonists who dotted the Mediterranean and Black Seas with their foundations. The migrants made no attempt to dominate the hinterland, but sought only to build a strong settlement on the coast to form a safe foothold and bridgehead for trade. Hence the 'city-state', for 'polis' in Greek means both 'city' and 'state'; hence Greek democracy, a natural evolution in a close-knit community; hence Greek philosophy, for dialogue and debate is easy in such an environment.

Greece set the pattern of city domination, but it was not unknown elsewhere. The Euphrates Valley from earliest times had its city communities, which in no way reproduced the developments which made the Greek states such generous contributors to civilisation and European culture. But the Euphrates Valley did produce the first great metropolis, to use the word in the modern, rather than in the Greek sense. Babylon was the first complex of human activity formed after the fashion of the great centres of trade and cosmopolitan life in a more recent world. And Babylon was followed by other great cities—Alexandria, Syracuse, Rome . . . .

They shaped the ancient world, and determined the standards of its thought and culture. It is not without significance that 'urbane' comes from the Latin 'urbs', a city, and 'astute' from the Greek 'astu', which bears the same meaning. With similar significance 'urbanity' meant fine culture in conduct, thought, and language, and rusticity' the opposite, unpolished ways, and crudity of thought and speech.

Christianity followed first the urbanised contours of the world which it sought to evangelise. It is surely not accident that the word 'pagani' meant in Latin the people of the countryside, just as 'heathen', its rough translation, meant the folk of the heath. In spite of some who dispute the etymology, it is surely reasonable to see in the evolution of the word 'pagan' from 'village-dweller' into 'non-Christian', a sharp reflection of the city-centred form of early Christianity.

It is not by accident, therefore, that the cities of the New Testament contain so much of the story of the book. The chapters which follow seek to set the narrative in the urban context in which it finds so much meaning and illustration. Those who carried the faith from Jerusalem to Rome saw their world as a network of cities. Of all the scenes of activity and witness which fill the story, only one or two phrases in the *Acts of the Apostles* envisage another society. It was a rustic scene on the Malta beach, the place where the shipwrecked men from the grain-ship found a refuge. Where else, save in the lakeside scenes of the ministry of Christ, and the villages of the Decapolis, is preaching elsewhere than in cities?

E. M. BLAIKLOCK

One

Antioch of Syria

THREE hundred miles north of Jerusalem lay the first 'city of refuge' of the Church, the Syrian Antioch. The great Greek city is first mentioned in the list of deacons appointed to organise the charitable activities of the Christian community. Nicholas, one of their number, was 'a proselyte of Antioch'. Nicholas was a Greek, one of the many aliens who had been attracted to the worship of the synagogue. The synagogue was active in Antioch where there was a large and ancient colony of Jews.

It was perhaps the influence of Nicholas which led many Jerusalem Christians to migrate to Antioch before the persecution which fell upon the Church after the martyrdom of Stephen. The new arrivals confined their activities to the ghetto, but Jews from Cyprus, who came soon afterwards, in a second wave or backwash of displaced Christians, adopted more liberal policies, and preached to the Greeks. There was considerable interest, and a strong Christian church emerged. The Jerusalem church, exercising its rôle of leadership, despatched Barnabas, himself a Cypriot, to look into the situation.

Barnabas, an intelligent and liberal man, was quick to see the strength and promise of the movement, and by one of the great historic acts of the past, he sought Saul in Tarsus, and established him in Antioch. A momentous year of ministry from two notable men rapidly consolidated the Antiochene church. Its first act of public policy was to demonstrate its unity with the Jerusalem community when the great famine of Claudius' principate fell with peculiar severity on the impoverished Christians of Judæa.

It was at this time that the Christians first found their name. Previously, where they had been recognised at all as a dissident sect, they had been known as 'the people of the way'. It could have been the well-known nicknaming and satirical propensity of the Antiochenes which coined the term. It is as likely that it was the invention of some city clerk of the Roman administration, who sought a classification for a new group which had come under bureaucratic notice. It thus came about that 'the disciples were first called Christians at Antioch'.

They were an independent group, who retained the mark and stamp of an early Pauline ministry. It was the church at Antioch which first initiated planned missionary enterprise. Just as significantly, it was the Antioch deputation which won from the Jerusalem leaders those vital concessions which made Gentile membership of the Church possible.

The great Syrian city of half a million inhabitants to which the harassed Christians fled, was three and a half centuries old. Alexander's vast and transient empire fell apart at the conqueror's sudden death in 323 B.C. After twenty years of confusion, the Battle of Ipsus confirmed the subdivision of the great segment of the world which the Macedonians had subdued. Alexander's general Seleucus, son of a noble named Antiochus, emerged as the ruler of Syria, the central kingdom of the empire. In the same act he founded the Seleucid dynasty, destined for two and a half centuries of life.

Ipsus was fought in 301 B.C. A year later Seleucus founded Antioch on the Orontes. The city was one of sixteen of the same name, for Seleucus seems to have revered his father's memory. Antioch in Pisidia, a future bastion of Rome, was another of the sixteen. In all Seleucus built thirty-seven cities. Seleucia, the sea port of Antioch, was one of two so named. Laodicea was also among the thirty-seven.

The place was well-chosen. The kingdom of Syria grew out of the old satrapy of Babylonia, 'heartland' of the Persian dominions, and it was politically expedient for a Greek 'successor-state' to establish a centre of gravity nearer to the sea and the West. Geography was thus consciously controlled to give the new foundation the Greek orientation which determined its character. Antioch was also an inevitable node of communication and trade. The horns of the 'Fertile Crescent' pointed down the valleys of the Mesopotamian rivers and the Nile. The body of the crescent had Antioch for its centre. Like Tarsus the city mediated culturally between East and West, and the fine port of Seleucia ensured that the trade of the old caravan routes, once the monopoly of Tyre, should find a western outlet at Antioch.

The Seleucid monarchs were cosmopolitan. They inherited that spirit and policy from Alexander, the first great internationalist.

Hence the encouragement of Jewish immigration. The Jews of the Dispersion, a wide-spread and compact minority, were a force to be reckoned with in the Middle East, and Seleucus attracted thousands of these vigorous and enterprising aliens to his new city by an offer of equal franchise. The Seleucids were enlightened men, and Antiochus I, who succeeded the founder, sought to make Antioch a place of learning. The sister dynasty of the Ptolemies in Egypt was to make Alexandria the intellectual and cultural centre of the Eastern Mediterranean, but Antioch was not without some claims to rivalry. Aratus the astronomer found residence there, and the translation of Eastern literature into Greek was encouraged by the court. It was thus that Berosus' valuable history of Babylon was preserved for the West.

Antiochus IV, surnamed Epiphanes, who reigned from 174 to 164 B.C., merits mention, for he won a notorious place in the history of Palestine. Syria at the time was past the high noon of her strength, and the emerging world-power of Rome had effectively checked the westward thrusting of Antiochus III, called the Great, in 190 B.C. at Magnesia. Epiphanes turned south, and by his fanatical policy of Hellenisation provoked the famous revolt of the Maccabees in Palestine. The events and triumph of that struggle determined the shape of Jewish nationalism for almost three centuries, and the vivid Books of the Maccabees are relevant reading for students of the New Testament.

Epiphanes, however, left other memorials than those of horror and folly in Palestine. He inherited the genius for architecture which marked his family. Part of his policy of Hellenisation was the beautifying of his capital. He built a great temple to Zeus on Mt. Silpius, and a lovely shrine of the nymphs by the river. He cut a fine boulevard, after the fashion of Babylon, right across the city. Trees, flowers, and fountains adorned this corso, and under the double colonnades the citizens of Antioch could walk for five miles.

A century later Antioch fell into the hands of Rome. The increasing anarchy of the Middle East had led to the intervention of the Republic, and the great Pompey subdued and organised the whole of the Middle East over the years 66 to 62 B.C. in one of the most remarkable political settlements of ancient history. Antioch became the capital city of the province of Syria, and drew notable vitality from the Roman Peace. The Jews appear to have drawn some shrewd advantages from the new régime, for Mark Antony seems to have restored their civic privilege, which had been lost in recent times of trouble. It appears that they were still prosperous and free when Antioch entered the story of the New Testament as the second metropolis of Christianity.

The rôle was in some ways a strange one. Antioch was a city of varied reputation. It was 'the Queen of the East', 'Third City of the Empire', 'Antioch the Beautiful'. It was also as rank in vice as Corinth. Great, rich, cosmopolitan cities, at all times, have concentrated and demonstrated the corruption of man and human society. Antioch was no exception. The outer suburb of Daphne, a pleasure-ground of parks and groves, the haunt of commercialised carnality, was internationally notorious. The place was named after the young daughter of the river-god who, said the legend, was changed into a laurel as she fled from the amorous Apollo. Apollo's statue, famous for the intricacy of its workmanship, stood there, and the god, not commonly associated with ritual obscenity, seems in Daphne, in consequence of the legend, to have become a patron of a vast Vanity Fair. Writing towards the end of the century in mordant satire on his own licentious Rome, the poet Juvenal names Antioch as the fount of some of the capital's vice. 'Long since', he wrote, 'has the Orontes become a tributary of the Tiber . . .' Or as William Gifford translated Satire III one hundred and sixty years ago, in the ebullient tradition of his time:

The Greeks? Oh no, with this vast sewer compared,
The dregs of Greece are scarcely worth regard.
Long since the stream that wanton Syria laves
Has disembogued its filth in Tiber's waves:
Its language, manners, harp, and scum . . .

And Juvenal proceeds to describe the lewd dancing-girls from Syria plying their base trade round the Circus Maximus.

From such a city the first organised missionary party set out to bring the Gospel to the Roman world . . . After Jerusalem fell in A.D. 71 Antioch became the centre of Eastern Christianity. From Antioch, Ignatius set out for martyrdom at Rome, and from A.D. 252 to 380 the city was the centre for Church Councils; and the Patriarch of Antioch, as the Church first developed a hierarchical aristocracy, took precedence over those of Rome and Alexandria . . .The modern Antaki or Antakiyah stands on the site, and there is still a small flame of witness.

Two

Damascus

DAMASCUS was a major inland junction on one of the roads which linked the river civilisations of the Nile and the Euphrates valleys, an ancient caravan route which threaded 'the Fertile Crescent'. To travel from Jerusalem to Damascus, as Saul the Pharisee did in A.D. 33 or thereabouts, one could join this highway at one of two places: near Lydda on the edge of the Palestine coastal plain, or at Nazareth in Galilee, reached through Shechem. Thence the road ran north of the Sea of Galilee, over the upper Jordan, and north-east to Damascus.

Alternatively, a traveller could bear right at Shechem, follow a part of the middle Jordan valley, make for Gadara through the Decapolis, and thence to Damascus through the dry and inhospitable Trachonitis. To calculate mileage is difficult, but by either route the distance was between 130 and 150 miles, a journey of something like six days.

Some notion of the distribution of population, and hence the nature of the two roads may be gleaned from the map. The road which passes south of Galilee, and through the arid terrain north of the Decapolis, is clearly the more deserted and uncomfortable highway. It was the road which touched or crossed the desert which always suffered the plague of robber and footpad, and the Trachonitis route was subject to such depredations. It was, at the same time, probably the faster way, and likely to be taken by a traveller in a hurry with a well-equipped party. Saul was in haste, or he would not have been travelling at high noon. He had also an escort. So the event which was to have a part in history took place, no doubt, somewhere near Damascus, where the half-wilderness of the volcanic Trachonitis merges into the green countryside for which the venerable Syrian city was of old renowned.

The quarry which the fanatical young Pharisee was hunting was the new minority in the Damascene synagogues. The high priest at

Jerusalem, where persecution had begun, had no real authority among the Jews of the Syrian city, but there was much coming and going between Damascus and Jerusalem, and some scheme of racial jurisdiction, connived at by the Nabataean ruler under whom the Romans had placed Damascus, may have made Saul's project of intervention and deportation a feasible one. The whole scheme was a typical action of the arrogant Jerusalem hierarchy. In passing, it might be remarked that, apart from the one reference in the second letter to the Corinthians, no other ancient authority mentions Nabataean rule in Damascus. A significant gap in Syrian coinage, however, confirms the arrangement.

Jews thronged Damascus. In the days of their strength and independence, they had never penetrated so far north in lasting military or political conquest. David appears briefly to have placed a Hebrew garrison there, and in the days of Ahab Damascus had to reckon with the power of her southern neighbour. Elijah had presumed to anoint a Damascus nobleman as king of Syria, and in Elisha's day Israelitish power pressed hard on Damascus' gates. But that was all.

Conquest is not always along the roads of war. 'Captive Greece' wrote Horace of Rome, 'took captive her fierce conqueror', and both Greeks and Jews in the first century were infiltrating the cities of the civilised world. In Damascus the Jewish colony was large and powerful. Josephus asserts that 18,000 Jews were massacred there during the great Jewish Revolt of A.D. 66 to 70. If the same considerable authority is to be believed, the influence of the synagogue was widespread among the womenfolk of the Damascenes. The Jews were a power, coherent and vocal.

Their synagogues rapidly felt the impact of the new movement in Palestine. It was an influence which was to flow north to Antioch, and then thrust westward along the old trade-routes to Cyprus, Asia Minor, Greece, Italy, Africa and Spain. The new element among the Damascus Jews called themselves 'the people of the way'. The term 'Christian' had to await the inventiveness of Antioch. The Jews and proselytes of the new faith had no thought of abandoning Judaism or the synagogue. They saw themselves as reformers, the spiritual heirs of more than one prophetic revival. They saw Jesus as the Messiah, but their protest against the corruption of urban Jewry went further back in history. There was a 'third force' in Palestine, on which the Dead Sea Scrolls have thrown some light. They were the Protestants of the wilderness, many of whom had found purpose and dedication under the blazing ministry of John. They would have been astounded to know what had come to Damascus in the hot afternoon with the stricken man who groped down 'the Street called Straight' in search of an address.

And yet, over the next days and weeks, they were to witness a pattern of events which, oft repeated, was to lead to the final severance of Church and Synagogue, and to the Gentile ministry of Paul. He was still Saul, with no thought of the wider name, when Damascus became the scene of his first ministry, the prototype of many another sombre but triumphant venture.

All the familiar elements were there. There was the place itself. Paul, as will be shown, always sought to plant his Christian groups at vital points of communication, power or culture. Philippi, Corinth, Ephesus, Athens, Rome itself, make the policy clear. Damascus, old as history and trade, stood at the desert's edge, in the middle of the inner curve of the crescent of rich land which swept from the coastal lowlands of Palestine to the head of the Persian Gulf.

Note, too, the sequence of events. A ministry in the synagogue, the inevitable bridgehead of evangelism, led to acrimonious disputation. The trained mind from Tarsus, schooled by Gamaliel, was more than a match for the Damascene rabbis. Plots followed, and the appeal to the civil authorities, a policy as old as Caiaphas. Save with Gallio in Corinth, the influence of the Jews commonly prevailed. In such peril, Saul fled. The indignity of it all left a mark on him, for a touch of annoyance is to be felt in the letter to Corinth where he described how the governor of Aretas sought to lay hands on him, and he made an escape over the wall 'in a basket'.

Aretas IV was near the end of his long reign. It extended from 9 B.C. to A.D. 40. He it was whose daughter had married Herod Antipas, only to be cast roughly aside for Herodias. Aretas' attack on the realms of Herod had incurred the anger of Rome, and a punitive expedition was averted only by the death of Tiberius in A.D. 37. Roman intervention was no doubt a rising menace in the mind of the Nabataean king, when Saul was in Damascus. Perhaps Jewish favour on the borders of his realm was necessary to his policy, and may account for compliance with the wishes of the Damascus synagogue.

When Saul withdrew 'into Arabia' for thought and meditation, it was into the territory of Aretas that he withdrew. There is nothing strange in this. Nabataean authority was temporary in Damascus, and in the regions of indeterminate hinterland which lay beyond, it was no great force, save in the cities and along the lines of communication. With the tension in Damascus relieved, Aretas would have no interest in a quiet refugee busy with books and meditation in some obscure corner of his land. Damascus is the northwest gate of Arabia, and in that forbidding realm are many hiding places. Saul disappeared, perhaps for a long period, and when he returned to Damascus it was with weapons of disputation forged, and a mind vividly renewed. T. E. Lawrence, whose dramatic revolt in the desert ended there, described Damascus as 'the sheath for his sword'. It was the place where Saul, soon to be Paul, drew his sword never to sheathe it again. Through Damascus he came back to civilisation. He was to transform it. It was a case of 'withdrawal and return', which Toynbee notes as a recurrent pattern of history.

Perhaps this time Saul could view the ancient city with a more appreciative eye. It lies in a long rectangle by the clear river, the Abana of Naaman's justifiable boast, the Barada of to-day. Many streams take their origin in the two great Lebanon ranges. The Orontes flows north and blesses Antioch. The Abana flows east, reclaims and irrigates a countryside which would have otherwise been sterile desert, creates Damascus, and then, its waters spent and exhausted, sinks into the sand. Its fate, writes the geographer of Palestine, Sir George Adam Smith, 'is a signal proof of how desperately Syria has been rescued from Arabia, and a symbol of the profound influence which the surrounding, invading desert has had upon all her culture and civilisation'.

Damascus is seventy miles from the sea and 2,300 feet high. Both are prerequisites of health and comfort in torrid latitudes. It is an amazing site, useless indeed for defence, but ideal for the interchange of trade, culture and ideas. 'Look east', writes the great geographer already quoted, 'and you understand Damascus. You would as soon question the site of New York, or of Sydney or of San Francisco. Damascus is a great harbour of refuge upon the earliest sea man ever learned to navigate . . . Standing upon the utmost edge of fertility, on the shore of the much-voyaged desert, Damascus is indispensable alike to civilisation and to the nomads. . . . '

Hence all history. The waters of Abana, flung in multiple streams on to the narrow plain, formed an inevitable site. From the earliest human occupation of the Middle East men congregated there. Disaster has swept the land but Damascus invariably rises again.

She was replaced by Antioch, and was subsidiary to that city until the Moslem conquest in A.D. 634. She has outlived Antioch, as she outlived hostile Nineveh and Babylon. Antioch faced west, and during the centuries of European domination in Syria was the superior city. Significantly, the Moslem elevated the eastward-facing town, and from A.D. 650 to 750, Damascus was a world capital, the seat of the Omayid Caliphate.

It was appropriately symbolic that the scene of the first active ministry of the Apostle of the Gentiles, should be this dynamic Gentile metropolis. It was a sign of the gathering twilight of the Dark Ages when Damascus, first of the great Christian cities, fell to the desert-based Moslems. Europe was in retreat, and the border city of the eastern wilderness was the first to mark the fact, the first sensitive point of impact when 'the outer barbarian' broke the Mediterranean frontiers.

Apart from the one historic incident, Damascus does not figure again in the New Testament. In the austere brevity of that account so much remains untold. The meagre narrative of Luke, for all the brilliance of his reporting, follows only the fortunes and the testimony of a few, indeed, mainly of one man. We should gladly know more of a congregation which could produce the gentle Ananias, and the enterprising group who so boldly organised the escape of the enemy who had become their friend.

Three

Tarsus, City of Saint Paul

'I AM a Jew', replied Paul to the Roman tribune, 'a Tarsian of Cilicia, a citizen of no mean city.' Paul was quoting. Poets' phrases are taken up by cities. 'Last, loneliest, loveliest', wrote Kipling of the city where these words are being written, and the tribute is remembered, as Athens cherished Pindar's 'violet-crowned.' But Euripides, the tragic poet, also wrote of Athens:

> *'Of no small note*
> *In Greece, there is a city which derives*
> *Its name from Athene. . . .'*

That was five hundred years before the Roman patrol rescued Paul from the Jerusalem mob, but Paul that day used of Tarsus the adjective which Euripides used of Athens. Had Tarsus appropriated the tag?

At any rate it marks his pride in the city where he had imbibed Greek culture, and acquired in youth those Greek habits of logical thinking which determined his priceless contribution to the New Testament. In writing to the difficult Galatians, Paul spoke of the purpose which had separated him from birth for the task of Gentile evangelisation. He meant that Tarsus was his appointed birth-place. The Apostle to the Gentiles had to be a Jew, a Greek of Tarsus, and a Roman. If that be not the fundamental meaning of Paul's words, as Sir William Ramsay wrote fifty years ago, 'the historian may abandon altogether the task of interpreting them, for they cease to have any historical application'.

But note. In Paul were integrated those cultural forces which made modern Europe. He was a Hebrew, trained under the great Rabbi Gamaliel. He could talk like a Greek and quote his native Cilician Stoics before the intellectuals of Athens. He could write in muscular Greek his splendid closely argued letters. He was by birth a citizen of Rome. At Tarsus only could one so privileged and equipped perfectly emerge. Set at a confluence of East and West Tarsus produced in balanced form an amalgamated culture. A group of Tarsian Jews had held the coveted citizenship for over a century. Paul could not help seeing the hand of destiny in the circumstances of his birth and education.

Tarsus, the modern Tersous, lies in the Cilician plain on the Cydnus, some ten miles inland. Such siting was originally a precaution against pirates, the ancient plague of the Cilician coast. To judge from the wide extent of its traces, Tarsus must have housed a population of half a million. It was a vigorous community, and the climate was probably more invigorating in ancient times than it is to-day. The lower reach of the Cydnus was navigable, and a port had been skilfully engineered on a lake in its mid-course. Smaller craft could continue up to the city centre. So came Cleopatra's barge, which, as Shakespeare pictured it, 'burned on the water', gold bedight and purple-sailed. It was at Tarsus 'upon the river of Cydnus', that the Egyptian queen first 'pursed up' Antony's heart.

Dion Chrysostom, speaking at Tarsus in A.D. 110, made some fun of Tarsus' pride in her river, and spoke critically of the city's environment. But the reason for the Tarsians' pride lay precisely there. They had dominated their situation, and tamed their river. It was their maritime gate. Their backdoor was an equally creditable feat of engineering. Thirty miles back lay the great Taurus range, cut by a canyon called the Cilician Gates. Up to and through this pass the Tarsians had dug and chiselled a major road. Tarsus was, as Ramsay described it, 'a city with its feet resting on a great inland harbour, and its head reaching up to the hills'. It was, indeed, 'no mean city'.

New Testament Tarsus had already a millennium of history. Its beginnings lie somewhere in the twilight borderlands of history, for one Mopsus was among its founders or first citizens. This probably means that Ionian Greeks, whose colonies occupied the western bulge of Asia Minor, came also to Cilicia, and joined a native Cilician settlement on the Cydnus. In the list of nations in *Genesis* 10, there is reference to 'the sons of Javan, Elishah and Tarshish'. Javan is certainly the Ionians. Elishah refers, perhaps, to Cyprus, and according to Josephus, Tarshish is Tarsus. This is intriguing. Tarshish, to be sure, is usually identified as Tartessus in Spain, but Josephus is not necessarily proved incorrect by this. The word might have more than one geographical reference. But this is groping in the dark. It is certain that early colonising Greeks came to Cilicia, and their coming is of supreme historical significance.

No connected story of the city can be given. Shalmaneser III, the

Assyrian conqueror, who wrote of 'Jehu son of Omri' on his famous Black Obelisk, also referred to Tarsus which fell within the orbit of his wide raiding. That was in the middle years of the ninth century, for the Assyrian's sanguinary reign was from 859 to 824 B.C.

Pass now to 401 B.C. over ill-lit centuries. The Persian Empire ruled Tarsus under a puppet-king. The name of this ruler was Synnesis in 401 B.C., for it is mentioned in a famous book. One Cyrus, a Persian governor from the Aegean coast rebelled against the Shah. He marched through Tarsus with ten thousand Greek mercenaries, and probably occasioned the deposition of the king for unavoidably aiding him. Cyrus fell in battle, and left his Greek army stranded in Mesopotamia. Xenophon, an Athenian soldier, told how the little force bravely cut its way out through Armenia. The book was to reveal to young Alexander of Macedon, half a century later, the intrinsic weakness of the sprawling Persian Empire.

When Alexander, applying the lesson, marched through Cilicia in 334 B.C., he found a Persian governor in charge. Greek influence was at a low ebb in Tarsus. This is revealed by the coinage, whose symbolic devices tell of the fusion and interplay of Greek and Oriental thought. Greek notions flood back after Alexander, for Cilicia became part of the Syrian Empire, ruled from Antioch by the dynasty which Seleucus founded. At the Eastern end of the Asian peninsula, Cilicia was an undoubted part of the Seleucid domains, not a wavering and disputed border-state like Palestine. Hence firm integration.

The region was ruled at first as a province, for the Seleucid policy was to discourage the Greek urge to city autonomy. It was only the shock of the encounter with Rome which checked or reversed the administrative plan. Antiochus the Great clashed with the Republic because his drive to the West crossed the borderlands of Roman interests. A dynamic Rome was feeling for a stable frontier in the manner which forms the main theme of her history, and Syria's Greece-ward ambitions were certain to attract Roman attention. The peace-treaty set Syria's frontier on the Taurus, with Cilicia, in consequence, a borderland. Hence a readier agreement on the part of the Antioch government on the question of Tarsus' autonomy. From this date, the Tarsus of Paul emerges, facing East and West, mingling Greece and the Orient, and vividly aware of Rome. Paul was the proper son of such a city.

But a vital date remains. In 171 B.C. Antiochus Epiphanes conceded an even larger measure of autonomy to the determined city. Unrest in Tarsus, in which the Jews played a major part, forced the Syrian king to act. A reorganisation of the constitution followed, and it included the establishment of a 'tribe' or ward of Jewish citizens. These were the 'kinsmen' to whom Paul refers four times in the *Epistle to the Romans.*

Antiochus Epiphanes was the savage oppressor of the Jews of Palestine, but that cruel and lamentable policy was because metropolitan Jewry rejected the king's ardent drive to Hellenise the land. He sought thus to unify his realms. In Tarsus the Jews were tolerant and nothing more strikingly illustrates this more liberal outlook than Paul's use of metaphors from the Greek games. That tolerance could accompany the firmest Judaism is also illustrated by Paul. There is therefore no historical unlikelihood in the suggestion that the ruler who persecuted Palestinian Jews, favoured the Jews of Cilicia, and integrated them into his social system.

Rome first penetrated the region in 104 B.C., but it was not until Pompey reorganised the East in 65 and 64 B.C. that Cilicia became a full Roman command. The great orator and statesman, Cicero, was governor in 51 B.C., and one of his tasks was the pacification of a bandit-ridden hinterland. The long Roman struggle with resurgent Orientalism, led by the remarkable Mithridates, king of Pontus, had spread anarchy and social breakdown through Asia Minor and the East, and Rome's decisive intervention was welcomed by men at large. The Jews of the Dispersion were an urban people, involved in commerce and finance. Above all others, they needed peace, and Pompey probably found the Tarsian Jews a useful force for tranquility and order. Their Roman privilege, passed by right of birth to Paul, was probably their reward.

Tarsus rapidly became the ancient equivalent of a university town. It was a resort of learned men, the home-town of Athenodorus, loved tutor of Augustus, seat of a school of Stoic philosophers, and a place of patronised learning and disputation. This was the atmosphere in which Paul grew up, and learned to think.

He also learned a trade, as did all Jewish boys. He wove the native goats' hair into a tent-cloth known from the province as 'cilicium'.

Here, too, was the scene of the first Pauline evangelism. Many of the perils and adventures listed in the famous passage of the *Second Epistle to the Corinthians* took place in Cilicia. From Tarsus Paul was summoned to a global task.

Four

Antioch, Pisidian Bastion of Rome

IT was probably July, in the year 45 or 46, when Paul and Barnabas, with young John Mark, Barnabas' nephew, landed at Perga in Pamphylia after exhausting weeks in Cyprus. In a score of words (Acts 13. 13, 14) Luke records the arrival of the party on the mainland, the mysterious withdrawal of John Mark, and the departure of the two older men for the inland city of Pisidian Antioch.

Antioch was a Roman colony and military base. It was elevated, no less than 3300 feet high, on a healthy plateau behind the Taurus Range. The journey of 160 miles would have called for eight days' arduous travelling, not without 'perils of rivers, and perils of robbers', as some tragically worded local epitaphs prove.

The visit also, it appears, involved a change of plan, and the change suggests a reason for John Mark's departure. In writing years later to the Christian congregations of the territory, Paul speaks of a debilitating and disfiguring illness which marred his first appearance among them (Gal. 4. 12-14), and of the notable kindness he received. Ramsay was the first to suggest a plausible explanation. In summer, the Pamphylian plain is a place of steamy heat, a vapour-bath like that which, in imperial days, drove India's Englishmen to the hills. It was malaria-ridden until recent times, and the readiest victims of the fever were the fatigued and unacclimatised. On both counts Paul was vulnerable. Prostrated by a malarial attack, he might reasonably seek healing and convalescence in the healthier highlands, to which those of Pamphylia's own people who could do so escaped in the dog-days.

For such purpose, it was not absolutely necessary to cross the range to Antioch. Or so, perhaps, Mark argued. A real change of policy was no doubt emerging. Instead of working west along the chain of Greek ports, Paul and Barnabas now proposed to make for a Roman colony. Did Mark withdraw in youthful intolerance, rather than acquiesce in the new plan, and thus cause a breach which took years to heal? Was a vision of imperial evangelism taking shape in Paul's mind, a project which outraged the younger man's firm Jewish nationalism? If so, Mark's later authorship of a gospel for the Roman world was a fine instance of mellowed judgment, with which his later intimacy with Paul attunes.

At this point the term 'colony' should be explained, for its meaning has varied in place and time. A colony in our own history is a settlement of citizens abroad, politically connected with the motherland. British colonies have tended to develop into independent states, and break the political link, either with complete severance, as in the case of the American colonies, or by their evolution into 'dominions' bound by links more tenuous. A Greek colony was an 'apoikia', and the word means a body of citizens away from home. The heavy limitations on expansion in their own peninsula, imposed by poor soil and the broken terrain, compelled the Hellenes to send their surplus population abroad from earliest days. Colonies date back to the seventh and eighth centuries before Christ, and their foundations dot the shores of the inland seas from Marseilles to Sebastapol and Benghazi. The Greek colony did not necessarily absorb or control the hinterland. Those which ringed the southern coasts of Italy, for example, from Naples to Tarentum, were city states, linked commercially with the land but politically independent, and contentedly so. Alexandria, to be sure, like Calcutta in another age, became also a bridgehead of empire, but the original conception of a colony among the Greeks was that of a transported population seeking only the rights of guests on an alien coast, but becoming inevitably a cell of Greek culture among more primitive communities.

A Roman 'colonia' was a device of empire. It was a transplanted fragment of Rome, a body of Roman citizens, commonly demobilised veterans, and designed to form a bastion of government in an unsettled countryside. Roman colonies were not necessarily new foundations. Antioch had been first established on the plateau above the Antios River about 300 B.C., with a purpose not dissimilar to that of a Roman colony. The Seleucid rulers of Syria, after Alexander's death, inherited from their Persian predecessors a trouble-spot in the Pisidian hill-country. Rome inherited it from them. Indeed the mountain tribe of the Homonodenses was not subdued until Quirinius was allotted the task as a special duty by Augustus about 7 B.C. He probably went on to hold the 'second enrolment' in Palestine, mentioned in Luke's Nativity story.

The Romans established the Province of Galatia in 25 B.C., and Augustus would not be likely to overlook the awkward problem of the unsubdued mountain tribes. One of the less spectacular achievements of his principate was the elimination of such pockets of resistance from Spain to Switzerland and Asia Minor. Antioch was a ready-made frontier community for him to Romanise and organise after the established mode. The most influential citizens would be elevated to the coveted status of citizenship, and perhaps be reinforced by immigrants from Italy. Without disturbance of the general Hellenic character of the city, Latin would be introduced for official pronouncements and inscriptions. Amusements, festivals, government, and justice would become Roman in tone.

A curious indication of this Romanisation is found in the late second-century document, the *Acts of Paul and Thekla*. Thekla, and the word is no doubt an abbreviation of Theokleia, was the daughter of a citizen of neighbouring Iconium, who was converted by the preaching of Paul, and became the apostle's devoted follower. She suffered shocking persecution, alleviated by sundry miracles. And in Antioch she was cast to the wild beasts in the arena. The girl had come to Antioch in search of Paul, had resisted a pagan high-priest, and suffered in consequence. The miracle tales of the savage animals which refused to harm her may be dismissed as the common stock-in-trade of such hagiography. The important and authentic detail is the *venatio* or 'hunt', a crude and expensive Roman exhibition of wild animals, here transported as a piece of Roman culture to the Asian hinterland.

It was perhaps late in August when Paul and Barnabas arrived. There was a synagogue of Hellenistic Jews, for in Antioch the three cultures, of which Paul was the perfect heir, functioned side by side. The strangers were invited by synagogue custom to speak. It was a composite audience as is evident from Paul's opening words: 'Men of Israel, and you that fear God, hearken'. In the synagogue, and the fact is much to the Jews' credit, there must have been a considerable non-Jewish element. It was this portion of the congregation which was so deeply impressed by Paul's sermon. There was a petition for a special address on the next Sabbath to a Gentile audience, and 'almost the whole city' gathered to hear it. There is nothing impossible, or indeed unlikely, in such popular acclaim. The modern world has seen as much. But Jewish liberalism had its limitations. From the account Luke gives, it seems clear that the Gentile proselytes were not equal members of the synagogue. There was a species of 'apartheid', with some Jews more given to integration, and some forming the too familiar hard core of nationalists.

Hence an open clash. An influential section of the Jewish community had close connections with the one group in the city which had not shared the popular enthusiasm. Among the Roman aristocratic minority the Jews probably had connections of two sorts. There were women adherents, for Judaism seems to have had some attraction for noble Roman women. The Empress Poppaea, Nero's wife, and Claudia Procula, wife of Pontius Pilate, seem to have been drawn to Jewish belief or ritual, and Juvenal the poet sneers at the cult in his Sixth Satire, his 'Legend of Bad Women'. It would do no despite to the text to suppose that the 'devout and honourable women' of Antioch, who were now roused against Paul and Barnabas, were such exclusive proselytes, non-attenders at the synagogue, no doubt, but recipients of the rabbis' ministrations.

The Jews probably had influence also with 'the chief men of the city', as leading business men and financiers. With the Roman element, male and female, thus constrained, it was simple to raise a persecution against the visitors, and cause them to withdraw to Iconium. Antioch showed Paul's world and the whole history of his century on one small stage. The Jews were divided, those with strong Hellenistic leanings, men of Stephen's, Philip's, and Paul's own fashion, and those of more rigid views, doctrinally or politically based, who, like the Pharisees, rejected all modification of Judaism, or, like the Sadducees, saw advantage in collaboration with the Roman authorities. Those authorities also ran true to form. It is fairly obvious that the charge against the newcomers was that their popular appeal disturbed the harmony and security of the state. Rome was always sensitive on this issue, and it was easy enough to precipitate hostile official action by mischievously raising it. It is an interesting display of a Roman colony in action. It will be seen again at Philippi. Note, too, the elements which made the population, coalescing or pursuing their own paths; the ruling colonists, the Greek multitude, the Jews, at one with their Greek neighbours over wide areas of life, but in a crisis prone to guard privilege with jealousy. Observe finally the disturbing intrusion of the new force, the Christian challenge, throwing into sharp relief all the hidden hostile ties, prejudice, and fear. The Empire was one day to react as Antioch did in that autumn month. It was a tragic error. Christianity could have provided a cement, a powerful integrating force, overriding all barriers of race and class, free from the taint of Roman dominance implicit in Caesarism. Rome, in fear and pride, chose her own cult, and chose grievously.

Five

Iconium, Damascus of Asia Minor

SHAKING the dust of Antioch from their feet in obedience to their Master's injunction, Paul and Barnabas made their way across the high plain to Iconium. The plateau, closed by distant mountains, has some of the features of a Central Asian steppe, and it must have appeared familiar country to the intruding Turks. From the eleventh to the fourteenth century, Iconium, or Konia as they called it, was a Sultan's city, and a base from which to harass Constantinople and the tottering Eastern Roman Empire.

The Turks boasted of Konia's beauty. 'See all the world, but see Konia', was their saying. Their medieval building of mosques, palaces, and mansions has covered up and hidden the Greek city which Paul and Barnabas sought as they trudged down the Roman road. Looted stones, perhaps with a half-obliterated inscription embedded in a Turkish wall, or sculptured fragments in cemented masonry, are all Konia has to show of old Iconium.

And under Iconium lay buildings more ancient still, for the city's beginnings are lost to history. Its name was probably a forgotten Phrygian word, but a myth was invented to give it a Greek meaning. King Nannakos, the story said, reigned before the Flood, and lived for full three centuries. An oracle had informed him that when he died all men would perish in a vast inundation. Nannakos gathered his people together, and so grievous was their supplication that 'the weeping of Nannakos' day' became a proverb which is quoted by a comic writer, Herondas, in 270 B.C.

It was in vain. Nannakos died, and the Flood came. When the waters receded at the command of Zeus, Promethus and Athena made images of mud into which the winds breathed life. So was the world repopulated. Images, in Greek, are 'eikones' (the modern 'ikon') and so Iconium found a name. This is what is called an aetiological myth, a story made up to account for an existing fact, name, or institution. There was doubtless a Phrygian legend of a deluge, as a story connected with Lystra shows, and the country was subject to sudden flooding.

There was an alternative Greek legend which dispensed patriotically with the Phrygian foundation. It told how Perseus came and vanquished the local population by the display of the Gorgon's head which turned all who looked to stone. The story is recorded on Iconian coins. There was a village called Amandra which presented Perseus with an image (or 'eikon') of the fatal Gorgon. On the site he founded Iconium. It is manifestly another aetiological myth which preserves as its inner core of fact the Greek colonisation of the district. Some scholars, without great success, have tried to connect Nannakos with Enoch, and find in the flood legend a trace of early Jewish influence in the area.

All that history can with certainty say is that an ancient oriental town was transformed into a Greek city by immigration. It remained Greek, for Rome chose Antioch and Lystra as its bastions. Iconium, to be sure, became a colony in the days of Hadrian, seventy years after Paul's visit, but that was when the colonial status was bestowed as an honorary distinction. Iconium was not a military base, but rather a city of commerce and peace, a natural centre of human activity, as its lively survival into modern times indicates. It is surrounded by two hundred square miles of good land, a pleasant plain, cool, well-watered, a tree-filled countryside in ancient times, its fertility the gift and creation of the mountain streams which poured down from the Phrygo-Pisidian highlands. It was, says Ramsay, the Damascus of Asia Minor, blessed like the Syrian city, an equally ancient foundation, with water, climate, and prosperity.

It was a Greek city then to which the two envoys of the Church were journeying, without the Roman social undertones of which they were conscious in Antioch. Claudius, it is true, was at the time bestowing some attention on the organisation of the area, and he had granted the honour of adding his name to that of the town, as London was once added to Derry. Iconium doubtless persisted over Claudiconium as strongly and as promptly as Derry survives Londonderry in its local habitat. The makers of coins, like the makers of maps, are more ready to use an artificial title than those in the street, and though Claudiconium appears as the legend on many coins, it is not to be supposed that Iconium lost locally its simpler name, nor its Greek character. It was governed by its assembly of citizens. Greek was the language of its public documents. Even the Romanised title appears on coins in its Greek form—Klaudiconion.

The two men journeying from Antioch were still, for all that, conscious of Rome. Roman roads were a tool of empire, and colonies were always linked by the famous paved highways which the Romans pioneered from the Tyne to the Euphrates. Antioch and Lystra were linked by a Roman military road, and this was the most convenient way from Antioch. Iconium lay down a side road. The travellers would almost certainly take this way.

At this point, the *Acts of Paul and Thekla* has something interesting to say. It is true that this document is late second century fiction, but it may contain some genuine tradition. Paul remembered bitter experiences in this region twenty years later. Writing his last letter from a Roman prison to Timothy, he spoke sombrely of 'the persecutions and afflictions which came to me at Antioch, Iconium and Lystra'. He added: 'What persecutions I endured'. Writing, however, to the Galatians, he had remembered happier circumstances, and much kindness shown to him. One of these acts of kindness was perhaps upon the road. A citizen of Iconium, Onesiphorus by name, heard that Paul was on his way from Antioch. He went to Misthia, the point at which the road to Iconium branched off the strategic highway, to find him. Like any host meeting a notable guest unknown to him personally, Onesiphorus was armed with a description. He was looking, says the apocryphal document, for 'a man small in size, with meeting eyebrows, with a rather large nose, bald, bowlegged, strongly built, full of grace, who at times seemed to have the face of an angel'. Onesiphorus found his man.

Paul, says the story, accepted the Iconian's hospitality, and taught in his house, perhaps in the open inner courtyard. The house was overlooked from a larger building next door, and thus it came about that Thekla, the daughter of Onesiphorus' neighbour, heard Paul's teaching from the window of her room, was fascinated by it, and became the apostle's devoted follower. The miracle-tale of the rich girl's sufferings was the consequence.

The pattern of events in Iconium was a familiar one. Paul may have stayed in the town over the whole winter, a ministry considerably longer than that which he exercised in either Antioch or Lystra. Luke covers the story, after his fashion with minor themes, in half a dozen clipped verses. Iconium had small significance for his major theme. Antioch had been the scene of an important statement of doctrine, redolent of Stephen, and marking a firm line of development in the subject of the book. Antioch also saw the historic 'turning to the Gentiles'. Lystra heard the first address to a purely Gentile audience, completely outside the Jewish tradition. Paul's approach was a simpler version of his speech on the Areopagus. Iconium was merely a link between important events for the historian of Paul.

It is possible, nevertheless, to gain some inkling of the shape of life and society in the town. There was no ruling Roman oligarchy, as at Antioch, to whom the Jews could clandestinely appeal, after the old manner of Caiaphas and Pilate. In Iconium the opposition gained its end by working on the feelings of the crowd, a typically Greek situation. 'The Jews that disbelieved stirred up the Gentiles . . . and the population of the city was divided, and part held with the Jews and part with the Gentiles'. Faction and division were common enough in the cities of the Greeks, for inability to compromise, and the mental habit of seeing all questions in sharp black and white were mental features of the Greeks, and mark for good and ill all their thoughts and history. Perhaps it was an attitude built into the Greek character by the sharp Greek sunshine with its clear definition of light and shade. Perhaps as fancifully, it might be suggested that ability to compromise, and see the grey between the black and white, is a mark of those who live in more misted, blurred landscapes. . . .

Riot erupted. There was no formal charge before the magistrates, but withdrawal seemed expedient. Perhaps there was a hint from the authorities to move on. Hence retreat to Lystra. Hence too the quiet return to Iconium and Antioch when other magistrates took annual office, and faction had died down. Such a return might not have been possible had regular proceedings in court determined Paul's expulsion.

Six

Lystra, Colony of Lycaonia

LYSTRA, six hours' journey south-west of Iconium, was another Roman colony, the furthest east of the strong points established by Augustus to facilitate the pacification of the south Galatian highlands. Inscriptions and coins have established the colonial status of the place beyond doubt. An undistinguished Lycaonian town, Lystra occupied a bold hill, a position of strength and vantage likely to attract a military eye. It was for this reason that it became a Roman garrison town, and a sister-city of the more cultured Antioch. An inscription discovered in Antioch in 1885 reads: 'To the very brilliant colony of Antioch, her sister, the very brilliant colony of Lystra, did honour by presenting the statue of Concord'. The words give the impression that Lystra sought rather to do honour to herself.

Paul and Barnabas came to Lystra to escape trouble in Iconium. Lystra was in a different administrative district, and it is unlikely that either Lystra or Derbe would have figured in Paul's original intention. He sought generally cities where a Greek culture was deep and established under firm Roman administration. Roman rule was firm enough in Lystra and the place showed some civic pride in its colonial status, as the predominance of Latin among the inscriptions shows. But in other respects Lystra was a more primitive community than most of those visited by Paul. Throughout the countryside the old Anatolian village-system prevailed, and the native language of Lycaonia was spoken. Lystra was the market-town, with the streets crowded by the local peasantry on market and festal days, chattering in their ancient dialect, bargaining in stumbling Greek with Jewish and Greek middlemen, and making way for the Italian burghers proud of their Roman citizenship.

The inscriptions attest the presence of the Latin-speaking upper stratum, although Roman civic discipline is not notably in evidence in the tumultuous events Luke describes. Latin may have been a symbol of the town's self-consciousness, and largely confined to official pronouncements, while Greek remained the tongue of daily parlance. Paul certainly used Greek in his exposition of natural theology to the crowd who sought to honour the visitors with sacrifice. It is the first recorded sermon to a Gentile audience, a kind of first draft of the famous Areopagus address, and it is interesting to mark the apostle's ready adaptation to non-Jewish patterns of thought. There must have also been some contact with the Jewish community, for Paul's invaluable friend and junior colleague, Timothy, came from this district (Acts 16. 1, 2). They were probably Jews of liberal outlook, if the mixed marriage, of which Timothy sprang, is an indication.

Even Lystra, then, showed that common commingling of race and culture of which Paul himself was a notable example, but it was the native proletariat, more conspicuous in this remote place than in communities closer to the main streams of Mediterranean life, which terminated the activity of the visitors. A curious legend explains both the emotional response of the city crowd to Paul's healing of the lame convert, and the violence of the disillusionment which followed the arrival of the traducers from Iconium.

Zeus and Hermes, the 'Jupiter and Mercurius' of the quite unnecessary transposition in the Authorised Version, were the patron deities of the Lycaonian countryside. This is indicated by archaeological evidence, which strikingly confirms the narrative of Luke. Two inscriptions from a region nearby may be quoted. They date from the middle third century. One records the dedication to Zeus of a statue of Hermes, along with a sundial, by people with Lycaonian names. The other inscription mentions 'priests of Zeus'. A stone altar, unearthed near Lystra, is also dedicated to the 'Hearer of Prayer' and Hermes.

In the story of the excitement at Lystra mention is made of the priest 'of Zeus before the gate'. In Claudiopolis, too, a town near Lystra, an inscription records a dedication to 'Zeus before the town'. The phrase is like 'St. Martin's in the fields', and suggests that there was a temple of special sanctity outside the gate of Lystra. The popular enthusiasm, however, might lack sufficient explanation without the evidence of a legend, preserved by the Roman poet Ovid, half a century before Paul and Barnabas sought safety over the Lycaonian border. Ovid put into polished verse all the stories he could find of transformation, from the change of chaos to order to

Photo: Trustees of the British Museum

Greek inscription from Thessalonica naming the Politarchs (*Chapter Nine*)

Thessalonica as it is to-day, showing the Arch of Galerius (330 A.D.)

Photo: National Tourist Organisation of Greece

Photo: National Tourist Organisation of Greece

The Acropolis, Athens (*Chapter Ten*)

Columns of Apollo's Temple, standing above a few acres of later Roman remains, are all there is to show of old Greek Corinth to-day (*Page 59*)

Photo: National Tourist Organisation of Greece

the apotheosis of Julius Caesar into a star. His collection, the *Metamorphoses*, became a Latin text-book for the Middle Ages and the Victorian school.

In the eighth book of his poem, Ovid tells the story of Philemon and Baucis who 'entertained angels unawares'. 'In the Phrygian hill-country', Ovid relates, 'an oak and a linden-tree stand side by side. Not far away is a marsh, once habitable land, but now the watery haunt of divers and coots. To this place came Zeus in the guise of a mortal, and along with him came Atlas' grandson . . . To a thousand homes they came seeking a resting-place; a thousand homes were barred against them. But one house received them, a tiny place, thatched with straw and reeds from the marsh. But poor old Baucis and Philemon of the same age as she, had been wedded in that same cottage in their youth, and there had grown old together. They made poverty light by owning it, and bearing it in a contented spirit. It was futile to ask for masters or for servants in that house. They served and ruled together . . . '

The story is charmingly told by the poet, but cannot be quoted in full. The heavenly visitors are received, stooping under the lowly door. Baucis throws a rough coverlet over the wooden bench, and puffs at the dying ashes of the fire, feeding it with her fine-split kindling. Philemon has cut a cabbage in the garden, and it is soon in boiling water along with a lump of bacon cut from a side hoisted up in the blackened rafters. A festal table cloth, kept for high occasions, is brought out, and the table steadied with a broken sherd slipped under the defective leg. Cream-cheese and eggs, nuts, apples, and dried dates, fill out the little feast.

The wine bowl, as it is emptied, fills of its own accord, and at the sight the poor old couple recognise their guests, and beg forgiveness for their humble fare. They have a favourite goose, and the trembling hosts seek to catch the bird to do greater honour to the feast. The goose eludes their shaky chase, and seeks refuge with Zeus and Hermes. It is an omen. The gods rise, and announce vengeance on the wicked district. They take Philemon and Baucis up a nearby hill, and before their horrified eyes the land is inundated, the little cottage alone remaining. And the cottage itself was transformed into a temple with marble columns. Its thatch became a golden roof. As for the good old pair, what was their desire? Philemon conferred with Baucis, and answered beautifully: 'Let us be your priests, and guard your temple, and since we have spent our lives in constant company, let the same hour take us. May I never see my wife's grave nor be buried by her.'

And so, says the legend, it came about. One day, long after, while they talked gently of old times, Philemon became an oak, and Baucis a linden tree. It was said thereafter in that countryside that 'those for whom the gods care are gods.' Ovid is a little vague about the exact locality, but one reading in his text could fix the site of the event a score of miles from Lystra. Geography is irrelevant in legend-lore, and 'the Phrygian hill-country' of the poet's reference is near enough. It can hardly be doubted that this Asian replica of the story of Abraham's strange guests and the Cities of the Plain, explains the emotion of the Lystran crowd. The gods had clearly come again 'in the likeness of men' with healing in their hands, to give a rebellious people a second opportunity, a Second Advent, so to speak, and a chance not to be missed. From the ecstatic cry of one imaginative man the notion would spread through the crowd. Barnabas was Zeus, Paul, the chief speaker obviously the herald and mouthpiece of Heaven, Hermes himself. The priest of Zeus-before-the-City was carried away by the gust of fervour, or else cannily seized a chance to canalise in his own direction the religious interest which had been evident in the town.

It was a strange situation, something to look back upon with a rueful laugh, had it not been so serious. Like crowds the world over the multitude proved fickle. 'Hosanna' readily turns to 'Crucify', and roses to stones. Paul came near to death under their passionate pelting. No Roman patrol came thrusting through the crowd, as it did years later in Jerusalem, to save the apostle from an angry mob. 'I bear in my body the marks of the Lord Jesus', said Paul in his letter to the Galatians, doubtless read in Lystra. Perhaps they were the scars of that day's savagery, when the peasantry of a little town found that their visitor was not Hermes after all, but only a Jew of Tarsus, a citizen of no mean city, but a man like any Lycaonian. Only Derbe remained for a refuge, and of that frontier town nothing significant is known.

Seven

Troas, Port of Asia

AT the western end of Asia Minor, lies a broad crescent of historic plain. It commands the entrance to the Dardanelles, the ancient Hellespont, the gateway to the Black Sea, round which the Greeks had their trading posts as early as the eighth century before Christ. On this fertile arc of land the Trojans, first tamers of horses, bred their chariot teams, and from their stronghold on the long escarpment, eight miles back from the sea, doubtless levied tribute on the traffic through the strait.

Since the amazing Schliemann proved, in 1870, that Homer's story was no myth, the archaeologists have cleverly disentangled a dozen Troys on the site, for three thousand years of human occupation have left their debris there. From the tumbled pile it is possible to look west and south, and understand why men coveted such a position of advantage. The far blue line of the Dardanelles is in view beyond the green, squared plain, backed by the low hills of the Gallipoli peninsula. Stunted oaks stud the plateau, recalling 'the oak tree' of the *Iliad*, round which many a contest raged, and making a link of strife and pain with Lone Pine, scarce twenty miles away, which marked an Anzac battlefield, three thousand years later.

To the south-west rises the island of Tenedos, a mauve hump against the sky. It was behind its shelter, the story said, that Agamemnon hid his fleet on the night Troy 7A fell to the Achaean raïders from Europe in the twelfth century before Christ. And on the sea-coast opposite Tenedos is another ruin, worn columns and well-preserved arches, which less-informed centuries took for Homer's Troy. Gibbon, indeed, wondered 'how anyone could confuse Ilium and Alexandria Troas', but the mistake was easy enough to make before the archaeologists uncovered the fortress on the escarpment.

Rose Macaulay, in her charming book on ruin-gazing, has described the raptures of Englishmen who visited Troas, and thought they trod on epic ground. There was William Lithgow, in 1609, who measured walls, and had himself painted in Turkish dress among the fallen stones with 'the tombs of Priam and Hecuba' at his feet. Thomas Coryat followed in 1612 with thirteen friends, and savoured lush sentiment for a whole day among grey columns standing amid the wheat. Coryat also 'discovered' King Priam's tomb, and the whole party carried off carved stone as souvenirs.

Ancient Troy, in fact, was near the end of her long history, when Troas was founded. The port was first built in 300 B.C. in the spate of Greek city-building which followed the division of Alexander's empire. It was a city of the Seleucid kings of Syria in the early days when their arm was strong enough to reach so far west, and then, like so many Greek towns, Troas asserted her freedom and independence. She maintained autonomy, or the satisfying shadow of it, under the kings of Pergamum who held sway in western Asia Minor, after wresting their domains from a weakening Syria, and even later under Rome. The port was of some consequence, the nearest to Europe in all Asia, and it no doubt suited the convenience of Pergamum and of Rome, to keep an entrance so important self-conscious and contented.

According to Suetonius, Julius Caesar toyed with the idea of transferring the government from Rome to Troas. Legend had said that Aeneas brought his refugees from Troy to found the Roman state and people, and Troas was near enough to Troy to call up sentiment in a people grown superstitious over the pollution of their homeland by the impiety of civil war. The project died, but Augustus remembered Troas and made it a Roman colony.

There the history of the town would end, or almost end, save for the visits of Paul. The first is described in Acts 16. 8 to 11. Paul and Silas had moved westward after an extensive tour of old fields of evangelism. They crossed from southern Galatia into the Roman province of Asia, but found themselves in some way inhibited from working there. The narrative is terse and tense in Luke's most rapid style. Seeking an opening for preaching, or for some liberty of mind, the two men passed into Mysia, and bore north for Bithynia. Another compulsion of the spirit caused them to turn west to Alexandria Troas. The Aegean now lay before them. . . .

Paul must have been strangely puzzled by the curious and compelling circumstances which had brought him to the Aegean coast. The port of Troas was long since a Roman colony, but the place was not an end in itself. It was a gateway out of one continent into another.

Once here, Paul found a guidance which he considered positive and clear. He met Luke, the physician, for 'they' in the narrative becomes 'we' at this point. In a dream, 'a certain man from Macedonia', as the Greek text literally runs, begged Paul to cross to Europe. Was the person of the dream Luke himself, whose persuasion by day was found thus confirmed at night? It seems highly probable, for Luke seems to manifest a pride in Philippi, and a casualness of phraseology in describing events there, which argue close acquaintance with the city and some loyalty to it, neither of which are inconsistent with Jerome's report that he was a man of Antioch.

It must not be supposed that to cross the Dardanelles meant stepping from one culture into another. Turkey straddles the waterway today, as Roman authority and Greek culture bridged it in antiquity. A man of Macedonia was not essentially different in dress and language from a man of Troas, which is another argument for supposing that the person of Paul's dream was recognised from personal acquaintance, and not by any distinctiveness of feature, speech, or dress. To go to Philippi was to step from one Roman province to another, but Greek was the medium of communication all the way.

From Troas the breeze must have been favourable, when Paul and Silas, Timothy and Luke set sail, for they accomplished in two days a voyage which consumed five days on their return. They ran past Tenedos and Imbros straight for Samothrace, and anchored for the night in the lee of the island's mass. On the second day they sailed north of Thasos, with Mount Pangaeus and their goal in full view. They anchored in the harbour of Neapolis in Thrace, and made without pause for Philippi. The whole incident is illuminating comment on the continuity of the culture, and the openness of the communications, which linked the two Roman colonies and made one world of the peninsulas of Greece and Asia Minor.

It is something like ten years before Paul came again. He passed that way after the uproar in Ephesus, and took time to found a Christian community (2 Cor. 2. 12). We should gladly know more of what must have been a period of notable activity and success. The scantily recorded period in Greece followed, which Luke passes over in the first three verses of Chapter 20. Eight verses follow about Troas, because the physician in Luke found interest in the case of the young man Eutychus. Perhaps he remembered that it was the healing ministry of Christianity which had first brought him in curiosity from Philippi to the Asiatic port.

But consider the scene. It was a packed and airless upper room, the atmosphere close and heavy with the smell of burning oil lamps. There was a high window-ledge on which the young man sat, and the hot fumes rose thick around him. Paul preached on through the night, hour on hour. It is a most interesting picture of a little community of Christians, eager beyond all thought of fatigue to hear the message of the apostle so briefly among them. Paul's power to grip his audience is as apparent in the rapid narrative.

Paul came again, perhaps seven or eight years later. The great fire in Rome of July 64 had brought the Christians into recorded history. Tacitus tells how the persecuted sect had become the scapegoat for Nero's suspected crime, the burning of Rome. Out of that act of fear and cruelty had arisen the imperial policy of repression, which the emperors were to apply against the Church with varied degrees of force and severity. Authorities, too, were to vary in the diligence or harshness with which from time to time they applied the law. In Asia generally the will to seek out offenders and repress was commonly more consistent and firm than in many other parts of the Empire.

So it came about that, perhaps in A.D. 66 or 67, Paul was apprehended in Troas, and, as a Roman citizen, was sent to suffer in the capital. Luke was dead, and he had no successor as apologist and biographer of his friend. Nor did Paul write an epistle 'to the Trojans'. In the last letter he wrote, however, the second letter to his beloved Timothy, Paul says: 'When you come, bring the cloak I left with Carpus at Troas, and the books, above all my notebooks' (2 Tim. 4. 13: N.E.B.). Why did he leave the garment at Troas? Summary and inhuman arrest, apparently, denied him the comfort of adequate clothing. It is a strange and poignant gleam of light on a great man's end. The last days of his freedom must have been spent in ministering to the little church, of which Eutychus was no doubt still a member, in Asia's most westerly port. Perhaps Paul lacked his cloak in the Roman winter, because to fetch or claim it that day in Troas might have brought the hostile notice of authority on Carpus, his host and friend.

Eight

Philippi, Colony of Rome

NINE or ten miles inland from the little port of Neapolis where Paul landed in Europe lies Philippi. A few ruins today mark the site. The town stood on the Via Egnatia on the edge of a great, open plain, one of the rare areas of extensive fertility in a broken and hungry land. Here on a natural arena, in a vital strategic locality, was fought the great battle which was to fix the fate of Rome, and open the way for the young Octavian to become Rome's first imperial head. Here Christianity came to Europe at the end of its first half century.

Philippi was founded in 358 B.C., in the first year of the reign of Philip II of Macedon. Founder of his country's military greatness, and father of the Conqueror, Alexander the Great, Philip was one of the decisive figures of Greek history. His ruthless programme of expansion ended the era of the city-states, gave Hellas by force of arms the unity she had never found by other means, and founded an empire which Alexander carried to the limits of the world, with incalculable effects on all future history.

Near Mount Pangaeus, inland from the northern Aegean coast, was a village called Krenides, or 'Child of Springs', named from its many streams. Here with shrewd strategic eye Philip built the town which bore its name. It stood on an eminence covering the approaches to Thrace, whose half-civilised tribesmen were a military problem in the rear of Philip's drive to the south. Above all, by the aid of such a base, Philippi controlled the goldfields of Mount Pangaeus, whose considerable revenue was essential for the sinews of Philip's costly projects of war.

Such foundations are an inevitable stage of history. Macedonia became a Roman province in 168 B.C., when Perseus, last of the Macedonian kings, was routed. The area was first divided into four districts, but the year 146 B.C. saw the organisation of a single province, through which the Great East Road of the empire, the Via

Egnatia, passed. This highway crossed the Strymon at Amphipolis, swung north of Pangaeus, made Philippi a posting-station, and reached the sea at Neapolis. Hence the clash of arms between Octavian with Antony, his associate, and Brutus and Cassius, in the war which followed the assassination of Julius Caesar. That was in 42 B.C. Twelve years later, Augustus, firm at last in sole possession of power, constituted Philippi a Roman colony, and settled it with partisans of Antony, his final rival, who were evicted from Italy.

A colony, as was explained in the case of Antioch, was expected to be a bulwark of empire. It was a replica of Rome, complete with magistracies and constitution. The citizen soldiers of Philippi had Roman citizenship, and formed a petty aristocracy. Philippi is the only colony of Rome named as such in the New Testament, though Pisidian Antioch, Lystra and Corinth, among the cities of Paul, were also colonies by constitution. In settling them at Philippi, Augustus was treating defeated troops of his one time ally and final foe with wise clemency. In return they caused him no trouble. Their privileges included exemption from the oversight of the provincial governor, immunity from the poll and property tax, and property rights guaranteed by Roman law.

Luke's strong persuasion may have taken Paul to Philippi, but there is no doubt that a Roman colony, a bastion of empire, and a nodal point on a great road system, would have appealed to him as a base for the gospel. A policy was emerging in his evangelism, and he appears deliberately to have chosen such points of influence, centres of diffusion, and strategic vantage points. There was no lingering at Neapolis, any more than there was at Seleucia, Attaleia, Perga, Peiraeus, or Cenchreae. Paul made straight for the inland town, which was, according to Luke, who must thus betray a personal loyalty, 'the first of the district'. Amphipolis was, in fact, the chief centre of that division of Macedonia, but Philippi's advantageous position was already bringing the town to pre-eminence. Colonial privilege and the vigorous activities of trade were more than a balance for the official title which the rival city bore.

It cannot be stated with certainty that Philippi saw the first preaching of Christianity in Europe. Paul arrived in the colony in A.D. 49, and it was about this time that Claudius expelled the Jews from Rome. Among them were Aquila and Priscilla whom Paul was to meet the following year. They were undoubtedly Christians. Furthermore, if the disturbances which Claudius sought to chastise are those which inspired the Nazareth Decree, as they are certainly those which occasioned a garbled reference to Christ in the historian Suetonius, Christianity must have reached the Roman ghetto before it reached Philippi. The Philippian church, however, is the first in Europe of which we have a full account, and a vivid narrative it is.

The party arrived in mid-week, and on the Sabbath sought the place by the riverside where a handful of Jews, too few to support a synagogue, were in the habit of meeting for prayer. Among them were some Gentile adherents, of whom was Lydia, the representative of a firm of cloth-merchants of Thyatira. As early as Homer references are found to the purple dyes of Thyatira, and Lydia was a seller of rich materials, probably a woman of substance. She was the first convert of Paul in Europe, and it was no doubt her hospitality which established that tradition of financial responsibility which was to be a mark of the Philippian church. She may also have set an example of female leadership, for Euodia and Syntyche, the dissident pair mentioned in the epistle, were undoubtedly two women of character and decisive opinions, not untypical of the Macedonians. There was a notable tradition of feminine freedom in the province.

Happy fellowship, fruitful evangelism, and firm instruction in the faith, continued for some time, if the solidity of the work is any indication of the time taken in laying the foundations. There were no Jews of any consequence to argue and to organise opposition. It was singular mischance which ended the mission. Luke never expands his narrative without a purpose, and the purpose of the detail which he introduces here is to set in its proper context of events Paul's first use of his Roman privilege of citizenship. A slave girl, whose mental abnormality brought gain to her owners, was restored to sanity by conversion. Hence a concerted attack on Paul and Silas, rendered the more easy and perilous in the Roman colony because of Claudius' recent anti-Semitic legislation.

Summary arrest, and imprisonment followed. Parts of Paul's world have changed little in nineteen centuries. To drive south today over the dusty roads from Chanak to Troy is to pass through country which is little different from that which Paul and Silas saw when they made their tentative thrust towards Bithynia. Thrace, across the straits, is another backwater, the more so at the beginning of the twentieth century, when Ramsay was busy with his archaeological researches. Hence the understanding of his writing. It is an earthquake-ridden land, and an Aegean earth-tremor, says Ramsay, sometimes behaves 'like a playful, good-natured sprite'. No one, he says, 'who has seen a Turkish prison will wonder that the doors were thrown open'. The seismic wave ran along the ground and passed like a giant ripple through the foundations of the gaol. The drystone walls gaped, and closed again. The doorposts parted, let fall the bar which closed the flaps, and fell back into place. Apart from the sickening sway and shudder, the prison was much as it was before, but the prisoners were free.

At this point the gaoler enters the story. The frightened man was probably a Roman, and could easily have been the grandson of one of the legionaries who formed the original core of the colony. There is nothing unlikely about his sudden conversion. Paul and Silas were well-known in the town. Philippi was not Rome, no vast metropolis in which a newcomer with strange doctrine was swallowed by the multitude and lost. It was also Greece, a land as eager as modern America for the spoken word, and full of open curiosity for the new and strange. Even in Athens the report of Paul's evangelism reached the ears of the authorities, and occasioned the invitation to preach before the Areopagus. The gaoler had no doubt heard the gospel, and needed only the salutary manifestation of the supernatural to precipitate his decision.

He had, moreover, retained the tradition of the Roman paterfamilias. His household was summoned to hear, and made no demur in following the lead of their head. The Bezan text, which often adds colourful details, inserts at this point an oddly Roman touch. Verse 30 of Luke's narrative, states that the gaoler saw to the security of the other prisoners before giving attention to Paul and Silas. It is possible that the detail is authentic, for, as Ramsay remarks, 'it seems highly improbable that a Christian, in later time, would insert the gloss that the gaoler looked after his prisoners before he cared for his salvation; it is more in the spirit of a later age to be offended with the statement that the gaoler did so, and to cut it out'.

Five verses later, the same highly original text adds another detail which, though not likely to be Lucan, possibly touches truth. 'And when the day was come, the praetors assembled together in the agora, and remembering the earthquake that had taken place they were afraid and sent the lictors . . .' The pompous municipal authorities, so proud of their Roman citizenship, were, in fact, in a most awkward position. Whether qualms over the earthquake had prompted investigation, we do not know, but somehow they had become aware that they had committed the serious error of imprisoning Romans irregularly. Paul does not spare them, and Luke obviously relishes the apostle's insistence on his dignity. Any student of Roman history who is sensitive to the atmosphere of the first century, must be conscious of the authenticity of the story. It is true that the praetors gained one point—Paul and Silas left the town. But that was, at this point, wise. The mob had been inflamed, and to stay would have been to press a notable moral victory too far and too imprudently. The authorities were, after all, not powerless, and the Roman citizen did not enjoy unconditional immunity. The sequel would have been a more regular charge, and a successful legal prosecution. As it was, Luke remained behind without apparent impediment, and the tradition of generosity to which Paul refers in both the letter to Philippi, and the second Corinthian letter, is itself some indication that the Christian community was not under official pressure. The church had, in fact, been solidly founded, as the letter itself suggests. Paul appears to have visited Macedonia, and by implication Philippi, on two later occasions, but no details survive.

One mark of the Roman colony is perhaps to be detected in the letter which Paul wrote, over ten years later, to the Macedonian church which he had come to love. It is a hidden metaphor from the chariot race. Exhorting his Philippians to effort and single-minded endurance, Paul writes: 'This one thing I do—forgetting the things behind, and stretching out to those before, I make for the mark, the prize of the upward calling'.

Commentators generally have not marked the fact that Paul appears to have in mind, not the athletic contests of the Greeks, from which he commonly drew illustration, but the chariot racing of Rome. He was writing to a Roman colony. He was writing also from Rome itself, and never was there such rivalry of racing colours, and circus fever than at that time. The common talk of the soldiers of the guard was of the chariot racing, and Paul would gain a vivid impression of this most perilous of sports.

Such a race as that which forms the substance of Paul's figure is described well in *Ben Hur*. The charioteer stood on a tiny platform over sturdy wheels and axle. His knees were pressed against the curved rail, and his thighs flexed. He bent forward at the waist, stretching out hands and head over the horses' backs. This is surely what he means by 'stretching out to the things before'. The reins were wound round the body, and braced on the reins the body formed a taut spring. It can easily be seen how completely the charioteer was at the mercy of his team's sure feet and his own fine driving skill. Euripides, in his *Hippolytus*, tells how the hero fell and was killed in such conditions. Ovid describes the same disaster in Book XV of his *Metamorphoses*. In his intense preoccupation the driver dare not cast a glance at 'the things behind'. The roaring crowd, crying praise or blame, the racing of his rivals, all else had perforce to be forgotten. One object only could fill the driver's eye, the point to which he drove at the end of each lap.

Of a Roman colony Paul expected much. A bastion of empire, and this was Cicero's description of a colony, could be a bastion of the faith. Paul expected intensity of living and found response to his expectation in the sturdy Macedonian church.

Nine

Thessalonica, Port of Macedonia

LEAVING Philippi, Paul, Silas, and Timothy followed an ancient highway for thirty miles, down to Amphipolis. Paul was probably aware that he was on Xerxes' old invasion-route along which Persia's marching multitudes made their great assault on Greece, and put Thermopylae, Salamis, and Plataea into history. Embraced by a loop of the river, and near a lake as large as Windermere, lay Amphipolis, rich in Greek and Roman history.

The district was magnificently fertile, and mineral wealth lay beneath the soil. The hills were black with pine, and it was easy for the travellers to see why this coast had been a bone of contention four and a half centuries before when Athens fought Sparta, and again a half century later when Philip, who founded Philippi, began his probing south. The timber was vital to Athens' sea power, and dictated the pattern of strategy, as the Baltic pine took England's ships north-east in Napoleon's war.

Perhaps Paul also knew that a namesake, Lucius Aemilius Paulus, two centuries before, had proclaimed Macedonian freedom at Amphipolis, when Rome's legions had ended the dream of conquest which began in Macedon with Philip and Alexander. Rome sought but to clear her eastern flank of danger, but she lay in the grip of history which thrust her on to empire. In Aemilius, Paul the apostle would have found much to interest him. He was an emerging type, a cultured conservative, just, religious, heir of two worlds. Like the best men of Rome, in the second and first centuries before Christ, he symbolised that splendid blend of Romanism and Hellenism to which Paul had added the vital contribution of Palestine.

There was, apparently, no synagogue in Amphipolis, and at this time Paul's plan was invariably to work outwards from a Jewish centre. The party moved on through beautiful country along the Strymonic Gulf, past the place where the great Athenian dramatist, Euripides, lay buried. Paul wept, says the legend, at the tomb of

Vergil, but no story links him with Euripides. The party moved on to Apollonia, spent the night there, and descended to Thessalonica. They were a hundred miles from Philippi.

It was probably towards the end of the year A.D. 50 when Paul reached the great Macedonian sea-port at the head of the Thermaic Gulf. The city had borne its name for over three and a half centuries. Antipater, who governed Macedonia while Alexander was absent in the East, had a son named Cassander. It was this man who, in 315 B.C., refounded and embellished the town of Therme, and called it after his wife Thessalonica, Alexander's sister.

The city was a nodal point of communication and of trade. It was Macedonia's chief outlet to the sea, a readier haven than Amphipolis. It stood at the junction of the Morava-Vardar route to the Danube, and the east-west road from the Adriatic to Byzantium. When Macedonia was united into one Roman province in 146 B.C., Thessalonica was the natural choice for the chief town. It was Cicero's place of exile, and Pompey's base in the Civil War. Antony and Octavian, the future Augustus, were in Thessalonica after the battle of Philippi, and it was they who made the port a 'free' city. Some of Thessalonica's surviving coins allude to the honour. There was a Jewish synagogue which served a wide area. Its presence in the city was, indeed, an indication of its central and influential position. A remark of Paul equally illustrates the fact. From them, wrote the apostle, 'the Word had sounded forth like a trumpet, not only in Macedonia and Achaia, but everywhere.'

The 'freedom' which Thessalonica enjoyed, with such cities as the Syrian Antioch, Tarsus, and Athens, was a privilege granted for good service to the imperial administration, as a tribute of respect for old renown, or for other considerations of policy. Such cities were commonly Greek. The status implied self-government within certain bounds. There was no garrison, and no insignia of Roman office were displayed as they were in a colony. Rome was meticulous in such formalities of respect. It was a device of empire, and much appreciated by the cities which enjoyed the fiction of liberty. At Thessalonica there was a popular assembly after the age-old fashion of Greek democracy (Acts 17. 5), and a board of magistrates called peculiarly 'politarchs'. The title illustrates Luke's peculiar care to name the various officials correctly in his narrative. Had there not been abundant epigraphical evidence from Thessalonica itself for the local use of the term 'politarch' for the city's magistrates, there would have undoubtedly been a charge of inaccuracy against the historian, and suspicion cast upon the record. The title is also found in a papyrus document from Egypt.

The events of Paul's sojourn in Thessalonica illustrate the constitution of its society. The visit must have been of longer duration than the three weeks singled out for special mention in Luke's account. It may have extended into the spring of A.D. 51. The Thessalonian letters, which supplement the brief historical record, suggest a considerable period of uncommonly strenuous labour. Unwilling to be a charge upon the community, Paul laboured with his own hands and received some aid from the generous folk at Philippi. The household of Jason, where he found hospitality, may have been part of a poverty-stricken ghetto. And a small one too. In more recent centuries Saloniki housed a very large Jewish minority, but this was composed of Spanish-speaking migrants driven out by the anti-Semitism of Ferdinand and Isabella. There is no reason to suppose that the Jews of Macedonia were numerous, or that Thessalonica, their chief place of congregation had a large or notably wealthy Jewish community.

Paul's ministry followed what must have seemed to him by now a monotonously familiar course. He expounded his doctrine of Christ, and, as always, anchored his teaching firmly in the Old Testament Scriptures. Opposition grew, not so much from the conclusion of logical argument and theological disputation, as from the nationalistic fervour and racial jealousy which were pervasive among the Jews of the Dispersion, and in the first and early second centuries led to some fierce tensions and bitter clashes in the Mediterranean world. It is significant that again Paul found his most ready hearers in the Greek adherents of the synagogue, and the upper-class women who seem to have been widely attracted to Judaism. To these devout and honest seekers Christianity offered what the synagogue in large part withheld, equality between race and sex.

But mark the reaction of the hostile Jews. There were no Roman magistrates before whom to lay a formal charge as at Philippi, the Roman colony. Thessalonica cherished a fiction of city democracy, and popular clamour, and the rabble-rousing activities of the demagogue, were always a blemish on Greek democracy. Like the silversmiths of Ephesus, the Jews of Thessalonica knew well how to rouse the city against the intruders on their domain. Their prime object was to raise one of those storms of mass emotion which Luke ironically describes in his vivid account of the tumult at Ephesus, and which the great historian Thucydides records in a famous passage about his native Athens.

The complainants had no true or formal charge to lay. No local right, ceremonial, or law had been contravened. Their hope was to alarm the politarchs, and so secure action in the interests of peace. The situation recalled a scene in Jerusalem which must have come to Paul's mind with both challenge and comfort. In most ancient cities there were idle crowds, dispossessed peasants, impoverished free men, whose labour was worth little in a slave-ridden society, the common dregs of all great congregations of men. They were the ready tools of corrupt politicians, and a social problem of the utmost gravity.

To hire the services of these wastrels was as simple for the Jews of Thessalonica as it had been for the baser Roman demagogues of a century before, as the Republic died in urban anarchy; as simple as it must have been for Caiaphas, when voices were needed to shout for Barabbas. At the head of their band of ruffians, the Jews assaulted the house of Jason demanding that their enemies be brought before the 'demos', or the popular assembly. This is what 'the people' of Acts 17. 5 means.

Paul was not found in Jason's house, but Jason himself and some of his fellow Christians were brought into the presence of the politarchs. 'These fellows', shouted the Jews, 'these seditious agitators of the civilised world, have found their way here also. Jason has received them. They preach treason, setting up one Jesus in Caesar's place.' Caesar, in fact, had recently expelled the Jews from Rome because of uproar in the ghetto, and the charge was slanted and dangerous. Again it resembled the false accusations levelled at Christ. The city authorities could see as well as Pilate saw on the greater occasion that there was naught substantial in the charges, but like the unfortunate procurator of Judaea, the politarchs of the Macedonian town were sensitive to any allegation which involved loyalty to the prince. The treason charges of Tiberius' principate were not forgotten, and the freedom of the city was a privilege appreciated and not to be lightly jeopardised for the comfort of a pair of itinerant preachers. Nor was it relevant, under the fiction of the city's freedom, that one of the two was a Roman citizen.

The politarchs judged it wise to 'take security' from Jason, and the device was effective. Paul could not imperil the small means of an indigent community, and the alternatives were inactivity or departure. The latter course was obvious. The authorities were relieved of their embarrassment; the apostle's friends were preserved from crippling loss, and the bitter leaders of the synagogue were left in secure possession of their petty advantages. But a Christian community had been founded, and its vigour, faith, misunderstandings, and devotion, are evident from the two anxious letters which Paul wrote to it.

That night Paul and Silas passed under the Arch of Augustus, and out the Western Gate of Thessalonica on to the Via Egnatia. The main road led to Edessa. Paul branched south and came to Berea on the eastern slope of the Olympus range. A few ancient remains mark the place where a pleasant little city stood. It was a long night's journey to this place of refuge, but it was safe for the time being, and off the beaten track. Oddly enough, Cicero, in his fervent speech against Piso, describes how that Roman governor was so unpopular that he found it wise to slink into Thessalonica by night, and then to withdraw from the storm of complaints which his presence occasioned, to this very town of Berea. As seclusion hid the Roman magistrate, so, briefly, it protected Paul and Silas more than a century later, They met the benediction of understanding there, of sincerity, and desire to hear, until the foe again picked up the trail.

Ten

Athens, Intellectual Capital of the World

IF Paul's ship doubled Cape Sunion, the southern tip of Attica, in daylight, the apostle saw what travellers still may see, the temple of Poseidon, god of the sea, crowning the headland. If a morning sun was slanting across the Aegean, to the north-west he saw a point of distant light, the sun's gleam on the blade of Athene's uplifted spear. Her colossal statue stood on Athens' Acropolis.

Piraeus is the port of Athens, a ship-haven on a blunt promontory four miles from the city. Here, no doubt Paul landed. For long years after the Roman Sulla's siege in 87 B.C., the port had lain in ruin. Forty years after the disaster, Sulpicius, the 'Roman friend of Rome's least mortal mind', as Byron called him, wrote a letter of consolation to Cicero in which he spoke of Piraeus as one of the notable tragic ruins of Greece. But another century had passed since those troublous days of the expiring Republic, and Piraeus must have shared the revival of trade and commerce which was one of the blessings of the Roman Peace.

In fact, there is some evidence that travellers did land there, as they do today, and not in the open Phaleron Bay to the east, which some have assumed to be Paul's landing-place. One Apollonius of Tyana, an itinerant traveller, teacher, and mystic, whose journeyings rivalled Paul's own, came to Athens about the same time as the apostle. An account survives, and the author mentions that Apollonius landed at Piraeus. Incidentally, he also notes that the visitor was struck by the altars 'to unknown gods'.

But this anticipates. Paul would walk up to Athens through the dismantled ruins of the Long Walls. After the great war with Persia in 480 B.C., Athens, newly aware both of her dependence on sea-power, and the emerging menace of Sparta's military might, had linked the port with the city by two great lines of wall, built by the whole population in feverish haste. The modern road follows the northern line, though nothing is visible to-day of the fortifications but a few stones on the waterfront. In Paul's day, for all the wreck the Sullan siege had left, much more must have been exposed to view, and up the long straight road the apostle passed through five centuries of crowded history. Lycabettos was a landmark before him, standing high above the city as it still stands today. And the Acropolis was in view above the city's roofs, with the Doric columns of the Parthenon picked out in the sharp Greek sunlight.

The life and industry of a modern capital have flowed over and covered much of the Athens which Phidias adorned, which Demosthenes sought in vain to save from the trampling of Philip the Second of Macedon, and which Paul saw in the days of her decadence. At the same time, among all the surviving cities of the Greek and Roman world, few so strikingly display to view the major memorials of a glorious past. On and around the Acropolis the bones of the ancient city lie bare. To climb through the Propylaea, the magnificent entrance portal, to the smooth platform on the great outcrop of stone, and to see the ruined Parthenon for the first time, is to experience one of the great moments of life. The mellow columns of the temple are so enormous, so exquisitely proportioned, so exactly placed, that every aspiration for beauty, solemnity and grace, finds satisfaction in one glance. Its shattered dignity dominates Athens still, and better than any other surviving remnant of ancient Greece demonstrates that sense of the beautiful, the balanced, and the true, which marked the Golden Age.

Paul saw the temple in the days of its splendour. The huge statue of Athene the Defender, which terrified the Goths four centuries later, stood inside the Propylaea. Another image of the goddess, gold and ivory plated, stood in the dim interior of the temple. The whole precinct was aglow with colour. The visitor to-day can only imagine what the total impression could have been. Grandeur and majesty still abide in the ruin. When the artistic achievement of Athens' Golden Age was still coloured and intact, the effect must have been overwhelming.

The view from the front of the Parthenon is a pageant of history. The island of Salamis is in full view, and the blue strait between. Here it was that the ships of Greece, brought to battle and inspired by Athens, broke the marine arm of Xerxes' massive invasion of Greece in 480 B.C., made certain that Persia should not spill into Europe, and set the stage for half a century's astonishing achievement in art, literature, and thought, which determined major developments of history. The triumph over mortal danger which that brave year saw, released energies in the Athenian people comparable only with those active in the life and spirit of England, when another Armada was scattered on the seas. Athens' 'fifty years', forever famous in history, set immortal concepts of liberty in the thought of men, and established patterns of art, architecture, poetry, and prose, which have not yet lost their strength.

In nearer view, from the same majestic vantage point, may be seen another rock platform on which the Athenian assembly met. Sadness lies on the grey stone, for it was here that Demosthenes sought by the might of eloquence to arouse to energy a people whose spirit had grown old, and whose genius had burned away. War had ruined Athens, the thirty years of exhausting strife with totalitarian Sparta, which closed her Golden Age and ended the fifth century. In the middle of the fourth century, Demosthenes, an unsuccessful Churchill, strove in vain to stir to saving energy an Athens marked down for disaster under the jackboot of the Hitler of Macedon.

Another assembly met on another rock outcrop . . . The visitor to-day can scramble round the ruins of the little temple called the Erechtheum and look down the northern face of the Acropolis. Below lies the agora, Athens' market-place, excavated by the Americans in recent years. There is little to see, save the traces of footpaths, shops, and colonnades. Here Socrates argued and talked. Here Paul, amazingly adapting himself to the dialectical habits of Athenian life, 'disputed daily . . . with any he chanced to meet'. But closer to the foot of the Acropolis may be seen the Areopagus, a small outcrop of stone, ascended by stone steps polished by the feet of centuries. To the right of the steps, on a large bronze plaque, in exquisite Greek lettering, is Luke's brilliant summary of Paul's speech to the assembled philosophers.

The Court of the Areopagus seems to have exercised some supervision over itinerant preachers, and the invitation to Paul was by way of being a courteous command. If Paul stood on the rock platform where he is reputed to have stood, he had the glory of the Acropolis in full view above him to the left. The graceful little temple of the Wingless Victory on its promontory of rock, the austere columns of the Propylaea, the frieze of the Parthenon, the Erechtheum, were all in the sweep of his hand when he remarked that God 'does not dwell in temples made with hands'. With Athene Promachos, and Pheidias' gold and ivory goddess two hundred yards away, he deprecated the folly that thinks of the divine in terms of gold, or silver, or stone 'carved work of man's devising'. It was splendid audacity. But Luke should tell the tale. It is reporting in his best style. Here is the passage from Acts 17, simply rendered:

> 'While Paul was waiting for his friends in Athens, he was deeply stirred to see the city given over to idols. And so in the synagogue he debated with the Jews and their adherents, and in the market-place every day with any he chanced to meet. And some of the Epicurean and Stoic philosophers met him, and some of them said: "What is the purpose of this picker up of oddments?" And others said; "He appears to be a preacher of foreign deities"—for Paul was preaching the gospel of Jesus and the Resurrection. So they brought him urgently to the Hill of Ares, saying: "May we know this new teaching of which you speak? For you bring to our hearing matters quite foreign to us. And so we want to know what these things mean". (All the Athenians and the strangers residing there spent their leisure in nothing else but talking and hearing about something new) . . . Paul stood in the middle of the Hill of Ares, and said: "Athenians, I observe that in every way you are uncommonly religious. for going about and looking at the objects of your worship, I even found an altar on which was inscribed TO THE UNKNOWN GOD! That which you worship, therefore, in ignorance, I am making known to you. God who made the universe and all that it contains, He, the Lord from all time of the heaven and the earth, does not dwell in temples which hands have made, nor is He served by human hands, as though He needed something, giving, as He does to all, life, and breath, and everything. And He made of one father every race of men, causing them to dwell upon all the face of the earth, marking out for them their boundaries in time, and their place of habitation, and prompting them to seek God, if perhaps they might grope for Him and discover Him, though indeed He is not far from any of us. For in Him we live, and move, and indeed exist, as some of your own Stoic poets have said: "For we are even His offspring". Being therefore, by the nature of things, God's offspring, we ought not to think that the Divine is like gold, or silver, or stone, carved work of man's devising. So the times of ignorance God overlooked, but now calls on all men everywhere to repent because He has set a day in which He purposes to judge the world in righteousness, by the Man Whom He has appointed, giving assurance to all men by raising Him from the dead". Having heard of a resurrection of the dead, some scoffed. Others said: "We shall hear you again about this". So Paul came out from their company. But

some men remained with him and believed, among whom was Dionysius a member of the Court of the Hill of Ares, a woman named Damaris, and others along with them.'

The address was magnificent. Those familiar with Greek literature and thought can have little doubt of Paul's competence in both. He quotes two Stoic poets, one a native of his own Cilicia. Even Luke's brief résumé has detectable echoes of Plato and Homer. The courteous approach, so proper to the occasion, is perfect; the homiletics are beyond reproach. Paul begins with common ground, a universal theism; he attaches his argument to familiar experience, the altar to the Unknown God; he bends his appeal to the more likely listeners, the Stoics; he talks the common idiom of his audience, and couches his message in their forms of thought. Here was the man who could persuade the Jews in the terminology and concepts of their ancient scriptures, with such intricate and symbolic argument as that which fills the Ninth to the Eleventh Chapters of the *Epistle to the Romans*, who could also plead with a Roman governor in the terms of his own living experience, teach like any sophist in the school of Tyrannus at Ephesus, and debate, like Socrates, in the agora. The capacity for adaptation is unique. . . .

Paul's speech was not a failure. One member of the court was convinced. The street which to-day runs round the south slopes of the Acropolis, is named after Dionysius the Areopagite. Others of the crowd, who stood within hearing, were also won to faith. Such a result does not spell failure, and Paul's words to the Corinthians, which stated his determination to know 'naught among them save Jesus Christ and Him Crucified', were no foreswearing of the cultured and relevant argument he used under the mighty shadow of the Acropolis.

And yet, be it confessed, Paul was lonely in Athens. His friends were not with him. There was no sympathetic community of Jews to give him a haven among his own folk. Luke dismisses the synagogue in a phrase. The brittle intellectual atmosphere was as tense and challenging as that of any University Common Room. It was no place in which to relax and enjoy a simpler human fellowship, had that been readily to hand. The overwhelming evidence of idolatry oppressed him. It was not all a scene of beauty, the lovely temple and the graceful statue. The 'herms' at the house-doors, and other symbols of phallic worship, were relics of the sex-obsessions which haunted primitive religion . . . Athens, no doubt, was a stirring experience. It always was, and still is. But perhaps it was with some relief that Paul took the road to Corinth. It lay through the village of Eleusis, where the great temple of Demeter, lost to-day in an industrial suburb, may have reminded the traveller of a saying of Christ about a corn of wheat. In the Eleusinian 'mysteries', the initiates saw their 'regeneration' symbolised in an uplifted ear of corn. On a lintel lying to-day in the tangle of grass and weed is a carving of such an ear. It is odd that, when Paul wrote to Corinth, his next city of call, he developed the image of the planted corn.

Eleven

Corinth, City of Two Seas

THE map explains Corinth. The most remarkable geographical feature of the land is the long arm of sea which almost cuts Greece in half. A narrow isthmus four to five miles across forms a bridge between the main land mass of Greece and the Peloponnese, its ragged southern peninsula, and the home of its most ancient civilisations.

Corinth, under the shadow of the two thousand foot outcrop of rock which formed its acropolis, lay on this slim waist of land. It was served by two ports, Lechaeum on the long Corinthian Gulf to the west, Cenchreae on the shorter Saronic Gulf to the east. The isthmus is cut to-day by the deep trench of the Corinth Canal, whose bomb-scarred banks are testimony to the vast importance of this vital bridge of land. The canal was a dream of Demetrios, ruler of Macedon at the beginning of the third century before Christ, and of the practical Julius Caesar, second founder of Corinth. It was actually begun and abandoned by Nero a few years after Paul's sojourn in the city. A 'dragway', or 'diolkos', linked the two gulfs in ancient times, for two hundred miles of arduous voyaging were saved by hauling the ships across. Cape Malea, too, the modern Matapan, southernmost promontory of Greece, was a notorious grave of ships. Those who sailed round its stormy bluff were bidden in sailors' sayings to 'make their will', and 'forget their home'.

The Corinthian isthmus thus became a highway of east-west trade long centuries before the Christian era. It was also a highway between north and south, the gateway to the Peloponnese. Here the Spartans planned their line of defence, abandoning Athens, when the hordes of Xerxes' Persian invasion flowed into Greece in 480 B.C. Valerian and Justinian, emperors of the later days of Rome, also built fortifications on the neck of land when breaking frontiers made old strategic patterns relevant again.

A city thus situated, on a node of land and sea communications, was inevitably destined for greatness. It was equally inevitable that she should be a city of the seas. Poseidon, god of the great waters, was worshipped at Corinth. In the eighth century before Christ, Corinth founded Syracuse, and the colony became a kingdom in its own right and a major maritime city of the Greeks. In the seventh century she founded Corcyra on the fertile island of Corfu, and the colony became, for brief and vital years in the fifth century, the third naval power in the Greek world, a pawn in the power game between her mother city, Corinth, and the dynamic rival, Athens. Poseidon was well served.

Ancient legend said that the Argo, Jason's famous ship in which he sought the Golden Fleece in the far corner of the Black Sea, was built at Corinth, and like all old myths, the story was a folk memory and rendering of history. It spoke of Corinth's pioneering of shipbuilding and the remoter sea-routes of the inland seas, and it is historic fact that triremes, the famous war-vessels of the Greeks, were first constructed in the Corinthian shipyards.

The trade of the port, land-borne and sea-borne, was prodigious. It was commerce which led to the clash with Athens in 430 B.C. Athenian enterprise had invaded vital areas of Corinthian interest in Corfu and on the Thracian coast. Sparta, the watchful and jealous rival, was drawn into the quarrel, and a disastrous generation of conflict, which history knows as the Peloponnesian War, ended Athenian greatness and burned something out of the Greek genius which the world was never to see in creative vigour again.

Corinth survived, and found it expedient to change sides in the continuing rivalry of Athens and Sparta, which dragged on, with sporadic hostilities, until the Macedonian conquest of all Greece in the middle of the fourth century. Under Macedon, Corinth knew some of her most vigorous days. Trade continued unflagging through all the vicissitudes of the city's politics, through all her activities of peace and war. Wealth follows commerce, and Corinth became the richest city and one of the most populous cities of the Greek world. Like all great seaports, she attracted the cosmopolitan crowds which invariably gather at the cross-roads of trade. Together with enterprising merchants, the middlemen of exchange, finance, and commerce, came the rabble of those who batten on great uprooted crowds, the vicious, the adventurers, the parasites of a dozen tongues.

Corinth sought, as great cities do, to cater for pleasure seeking multitudes with money to spend. The flat summit of the Acrocorinthus, the acropolis of the isthmus, housed the temple of Aphrodite with its priestess courtesans, whose activities in the crowded streets were the last degeneracy of some fertility cult. Such corruption went far to make a background for the organised and commercialised vice which made Corinth so notorious a centre of carnality and the base pursuit of pleasure that the Greek language made a verb of the city's name. 'Korinthiazesthai' meant, in the downright language of Liddell and Scott's Greek Lexicon, 'to practice whoredom', while the word 'Corinthian' penetrated as far as the slang of Regency England as a term for a polished rake. 'Maritime cities', wrote Cicero gravely, 'suffer corruption and degeneration of morals, for they receive a mixture of strange languages and customs, and import foreign ways as well as foreign merchandise'. The great orator then proceeded to name Corinth and Carthage, both huge commercial city-states, which suffered catastrophic overthrow almost at the same time.

Disaster came to Corinth in 146 B.C. The city, in a final inglorious hour of political leadership, had headed a league of southern Greek states against Rome. It was ironical that it was at Corinth, fifty years before, that Rome had sought to reconstitute Greek freedom. Rome had been drawn into conflict with Macedon as a sequel to the generation-long conflict with the African Phoenician city of Carthage, which closed the second century before Christ. She subdued Macedon, and in 194 B.C., not seeking empire and costly eastward expansion, decided to withdraw from Greece. Amid scenes of wild enthusiasm at Corinth, Flamininus the Roman commander, proclaimed Greek liberty and the evacuation of all Roman garrisons. 'Now that you have full liberty', he told the Greeks, 'show that you understand its value by maintaining peace and goodwill among yourselves. Let the Roman people know you are worthy of the gift they have bestowed'.

Greece, decadent and faction-ridden, and weakened by two centuries of Macedonian imperialism, was not worthy. The events of the half century during which Rome was drawn deeper and deeper into Greece, the Aegean, and Asia, need not be traversed. The crisis for Corinth came with a foolish challenge to Rome. In 146 B.C. the consul Mummius took the city with small effort, sacked it and utterly destroyed it, massacring and enslaving its inhabitants. All its treasures of art or wealth were seized. The Greeks, with little left to cheer them in this last day of their shame, quoted with malice

Mummius' direction to the shipmen who transported priceless works of art to Rome that any items lost 'must be replaced with pieces of equal value'. Soldiers used a fine canvas of Aristides as a gaming board. A few columns of Apollo's temple, standing above a few acres of later Roman remains, are all there is to show of old Greek Corinth today.

For a century the historic site lay waste. Servius Sulpicius, the 'Roman friend of Rome's least mortal mind', described a voyage he made in 50 B.C. on the Saronic Gulf. He sought to console his friend Cicero for the death of his daughter. 'Alas', he said, 'that we should grieve for fragile human lives, when round about us the corpses of great cities lie' . . . 'Sailing towards Megara, I began to survey the regions round about . . . Piraeus lay upon my right and Corinth on the left, towns which once were prosperous and now lie in ruin or decay. . . .'

Five years later Julius Caesar raised Corinth from the dust. He settled demobilised soldiers there, and rebuilt the city. Merchants flocked back. Jews of the Dispersion came in numbers. The incomparable site exerted its old magnetism, and the city boomed. Old evil raised its head, as though Corinth had slept, not died, upon its crowded isthmus. Again its carnality, its sin, its brash new life, became a proverb in the Mediterranean.

The new Corinth was a century old when Paul sailed west from Athens in A.D. 51. The cities are only forty-five miles apart, and Athens' Acropolis can be descried from the peak of Corinth's citadel where Aphrodite's temple stood. Piraeus and Corinth were sharing richly in the trade which came with the Roman Peace. The isthmus roared with life, and Corinth was the seat of the Roman proconsul. Perhaps that was fortunate.

Paul sought refuge with fellow-craftsmen. Three years before, Claudius had expelled the Jewish community of Rome. Aquila and Priscilla, a much travelled couple, makers of tent-cloth by trade, had carried their craft to Corinth. Paul was also a weaver of Cilician cloth. Like every rabbi he had a handicraft, for the law had set its face against the commercialisation of instruction, and sought at least a token that no teacher of the Jews battened on the pupils who sat under him. Gifts replaced salary and fees, but a gesture at least was made.

Settling by the synagogue Paul plied his trade. He was ill, as the second chapter of the first letter he wrote to Corinth shows, and in the weakness of his condition lacked all confidence. From the motley mass of Corinth's population he nevertheless won converts. They were as varied as the city's multitude, courtesans from Aphrodite's shrine, dregs from the slums, as well as such men and women of standing as Crispus, one-time head of the Jewish community, Erastus, the city treasurer, and the well-to-do lady Chloe from Cenchreae. At the same time, as Paul later remarked, chilling the philosophic pretensions of a vocal group, 'not many mighty, not many high-born, not many wise' came into the church. He reminded them in the same letter that 'no fornicator or idolater, none who are guilty of either adultery or sexual perversion, no thieves, or drunkards, or slanderers or swindlers' can find acceptance, adding astonishingly: 'Such were some of you'.

The old pattern of Jewish opposition, sickeningly familiar, was repeated, but this time the persecutors overreached themselves. Gallio, kindly and gentle brother of Seneca, the Roman statesman, philosopher, writer, and millionaire, who was to guide so wisely the early years of Nero, and finally to die at that tyrant's hand, became governor of Achaea. Both Seneca and Statius the poet testify to Gallio's sweetness of disposition. Perhaps the synagogue hoped to bully such a man. Paul was hustled before his judgment-seat, but when the Roman heard the charge he refused to adjudicate. He was no Pilate, compromised by past mistakes, no Festus, under orders at all costs to conciliate collaborators in an explosive situation. He saw no case to judge, and turned a blind eye when the turbulent Greeks chastised the dishonest litigants. The story is told in full by Luke, who saw in it another legal vindication of the Christian's right to preach.

Paul thus continued with the Jews daunted and abashed. The founding of a church in such a place was one of the triumphs of his life. The faults of the town invaded the Christian community and it was ever in peril of faction, loose living, litigious intolerance, and philosophic aberration. All this may be read in the Corinthian letters. The problem of the trade-guilds, which will be met again at Ephesus, was acute, as puzzled Christians sought some means of compromise in an atmosphere which reeked of paganism. The imagery of the letters is vivid with details of Corinthian life. The Isthmian Games, second only to the Olympic, were held at Corinth, and provided metaphors from boxing and the race. The long-haired dandies, the polished bronze mirrors which Corinth manufactured, a Roman triumph, the theatre, the well-remembered judgment-seat of the proconsul, builders, architects, all these facets of life colour Paul's language. Two years almost had slipped by before he took ship for Syria. Paul had few periods as toilsome and as fruitful. From Philippi to the Isthmus, Greece had been an astonishing experience.

Twelve

Ephesus, City of Artemis

EPHESUS was already at least ten centuries old when Paul first trod the marble paving-stones of the fine street which ran from the harbour on the Cayster's mouth to the Great Theatre, where the level land began to rise towards Mount Pion. It was a boulevard of some magnificence lined by columned porticoes and fine buildings, the fitting seaward end of the long trade route of the Cayster valley and the lands beyond. It was later to be even more richly adorned. For Ephesus itself it formed a main artery where life and activity were channelled.

If a phrase in Beza's text of the New Testament is authentic, a glimpse is caught of the city's movement in excited action there. Beza's unorthodox text often adds an illuminating comment which may contain the truth, and Acts 19. 28 provides an illustration. It gives one brief camera-shot of the scene in Ephesus as the great riot began. Inflamed by the speech of the rabble-rouser Demetrius, no doubt delivered in the regular meeting-house of the silversmiths' guild, the audience, says Beza's version, poured 'into the street'. It is easy to picture the scene. Gathering the flotsam of the town on its wave, and sweeping along with it the idle and the curious, the mob flowed to the city's place of common assembly, the Great Theatre . . . It was a less passionate crowd through which Paul threaded his way in Ephesus as he journeyed from Corinth to Antioch. The lamentable scene in the assembly was three years away.

Much was to happen in that time . . . Paul used his brief visit to address the synagogue, a large one, for there were many Jews in Ephesus. He left behind Aquila and Priscilla, that competent and much-travelled pair, to found a church, and went on to Syria. In a few months he returned, this time by land, and fresh from a tour of the Christian communities in Galatia and Phrygia. He reasoned with the Jews patiently for three months, and then, turning, as he had so often done, to a more responsive audience, for a space of two years he taught in the hired school-room of one Tyrannus.

The results were momentous. All Asia heard, and a crop of churches sprang up which later formed the circuit of John, Paul's brother apostle. The city itself felt the impact. There was a grand burning of books of magic, like the bonfire in Savonarola's Florence, as converts to Paul's teaching sought to symbolise in public their abandonment of old superstitions and the degrading practice of occult arts and rituals. It was thus that Paul came into collision with the worshippers of Artemis, the 'Diana of the Ephesians' familiar from the Latinised name in the Authorised Version.

To understand that situation an excursion into history is necessary. When Greek colonists settled at the mouth of the Cayster valley in the tenth, or as some say, the twelfth century before Christ, they found among the primitive Anatolian population of the region the cult of a nature-goddess, associated probably with fertility rituals, and cherishing as a cult object a meteoric stone, the 'image which fell down from Zeus' of the guild-master's clever speech. Lost somewhere in the ruins of Ephesus, or concealed in the hills by its last devotees, the sacred stone probably still exists. On to this barbarous worship the Greek colonists, in typical Greek fashion, grafted the worship of the huntress-virgin Artemis. Other influences intruded, and the final form of Artemis' cult-image was a strangely ornamented figure with its upper half hung with bunches of dates, or, as some thought, with incongruously multiple breasts.

When the first temple was built for the goddess is not known. It was burned in 365 B.C. Its successor was the famous shrine some of whose green columns may still be seen, built into Justinian's Saint Sophia at Istanbul. Counted one of 'the seven wonders of the world', it endured until the Goths sacked Ephesus in A.D. 263. The ruins were identified in a marsh, one and a half miles north east of the city, after some clever sleuthing and the discovery of Ephesus' main street by J. T. Wood in 1870. The marvel is that a building so famed and so magnificent could vanish. It was four times the size of Athens' Parthenon. It was adorned by the sculptors Pheidias and Praxiteles, and the painter Apelles, and was fabulously rich with the votive offerings of Asia. It was widely depicted on coins, which go some way to justify the guildmaster's hyperbole that 'Asia and the whole world' revered Artemis. Ruined by raiding Goths, plundered by temple and church-building emperors, the great shrine was slowly destroyed. Justinian built a church to Saint John on the site. The apostle was called in Greek 'Hagios Theologos'—'the Holy Theologian'. This, corrupted into Ayasoluk, gave the village on the site its modern Turkish name.

When Paul stirred the city with his teaching in the school of Tyrannus, the worship of Artemis was the city's most important industry. The great days of Ephesian trade were past. Like Miletus at the end of the Maeander valley thirty miles south, Ephesus was silting up its harbour. It is the old folly of man to strip the forests from the hills. Axe and fire, and the destructiveness of the goat, familiar domestic animal of the Mediterranean peasantry, had denuded the wooded hills of Asia Minor. Topsoil had slipped in the winter rains, streams had choked, and the silt-laden flood-waters had filled the harbours. The harbour works of Ephesus may be traced to-day seven miles from the sea. Where once the little gulf and waterway sheltered the ships, there is now a reedy plain where the rustling fen-grass raises a long uncanny whisper in the evening wind.

Over many centuries Ephesus was fortunate in its engineers. The Maeander was silting up the harbour of Miletus as early as 500 B.C., and when that city suffered damage in the Persian suppression of the Ionian Greek revolt, the choking of the waterway passed beyond control and remedy. Trade was deflected to Ephesus, and a series of rulers promoted the maintenance of the city's harbour facilities. The kings of Pergamum, one of the successor states of Alexander's empire, did much for the port, and the Romans followed suit. They inherited the kingdom in 133 B.C. by the will of its last ruler, Attalus III, who sought thus to preserve his little land from the misery of dynastic strife, and saw perhaps that the Roman defeat of Seleucid Syria, sixty years before, had marked the dynamic people of the Tiber city as the future masters of the Mediterranean. The Romans used Ephesus as the proconsul's seat, and the gateway to Asia. The city was proud of its name, 'the Landing Place', and the title is found on a coin as late as the third century. It is significant that the same coin shows a small oar-propelled ship, an official's 'barge', not the deep-hulled merchant ships which celebrated Ephesus' trade on coins in earlier centuries. Domitian, at the end of the first century, was the last ruler to repair the harbour of Ephesus, but long before his time trade had sadly declined.

Ephesus had turned, as any country would in such a situation of economic depression, to her tourist trade. Multitudes came to visit

Photo: J. Allan Cash

Remains of marble street in the ruins of Ephesus (*Page 67*)

Roman aqueduct near Caesarea (*Page 73*)

Photo: J. Allan Cash

The Damascus Gate, Jerusalem (*Chapter Fifteen*)

Photo: J. Allan Cash

Picturesque Roman remains at Caesarea (*Chapter Fourteen*)

Photo: J. Allan Cash

the temple of Artemis, and took away with them silver models of the shrine which had become a major source of revenue in the city. Paul's preaching against idolatry hit the trade hard. Hence the riot in the theatre, so vividly and ironically described by Luke. It is a strong clear light on the manner in which Christianity was cutting across established patterns of pagan living. Seventy years later in Bithynia, if we read aright two letters of the Roman governor Pliny, the Christian minority in like fashion affected the butchers' livelihood and their sale of meat from the temple altars. Repression similarly resulted.

So it came about that Paul 'fought with wild beasts at Ephesus'. The howling mob chanting 'megalê hê Artemis tôn Ephesiôn' was like a pack of wolves. It required all the political art of the *grammateus*, no 'town-clerk', but the city's leading official—to restore quiet and order. One phrase in his clever oration perhaps dates the incident. If aught illegal had been done, he said, 'there are proconsuls'. Why the plural? Tacitus tells how Agrippina, the vicious mother of Nero, had the proconsul of Asia poisoned when her son succeeded to the purple. Junius Silanus was the great-grandson of Augustus, and there were those who coupled his name with open scorn for the boy who had so wickedly been thrust into imperial authority. The murder was committed by two men, a Roman knight and a freedman who administered the emperor's estates in Asia. If these villains assumed temporary proconsular authority, the plural is accounted for, and the date fixed. It must have been A.D. 54.

There is another curious phrase in the story. Why did 'certain of the chief of Asia' seek to protect Paul? These 'Asiarchs' were members of a corporation, built on an earlier Greek model in the area, and set up to organise the Caesar-cult in Ephesus. Perhaps there [illegible]as rivalry between the stewards of the still modest ritual by which [illegible] worship of Rome and the emperor was conducted, and the [illegible]nboyant commercialised cult of Artemis. Perhaps they were not [illegible]y to see a blow struck against the rival. Perhaps also, with some [illegible]e of loyalty, they sought to protect a Roman citizen. The [illegible]rence is a puzzle. But one fact emerges from the story, and that [illegible]e tremendous impact of one man's teaching on a city of 300,000 [illegible]le. The pagan material of the great religious capital of Asia [illegible]t have been tinder-dry for the spark and flame of something [illegible] pure and noble. Asia had suffered much under the exploitation [illegible]ne dying Republic. When the autocracy called the Empire emerged from the ruins of the Republic, Asia shared the peace and just administration which the new régime gave to the world. Hence the reaching out for a new form of worship to give such gratitude expression. Perhaps for some the process was a catalyst, breaking down old paganism, but giving no true satisfaction. To such, Christianity came with power.

Paul withdrew after the riot. Three or four years later he passed along the coast without calling at the city. He invited the leaders of the church to meet him at Miletus, and from the intimacy of three years' experience of their community he warned them of tensions to come. They came, and a letter of John is the witness. John became the leader of the Ephesian church, and when he was in Patmos during Domitian's persecution, he addressed cryptic letters to seven of the churches of Asia. It was prudent to write in the style of Hebrew apocalyptic literature.

Ephesus, as was proper, was the first church addressed. The letter reveals that Paul's forebodings were well-founded. There was much to commend the church, which is thus glimpsed a generation from its foundation. Three years in the school of Tyrannus had laid a firm base. But the weariness of a declining city had seeped into the church, and the spirit of compromise which had been an instinct in the city's artificial and curiously mingled religious life, had produced the group known as the Nicolaitans, who sought for some means of accommodation with the pagan environment. Of this group we should gladly know more. They were probably Greek converts who saw their own mystery cults as a species of preparation for Christianity, and looked with a kindlier eye than either Paul or John would have sanctioned on the practice and ritual of pagan cults. It is true that in the religions of the Mediterranean world there was a core of spiritual truth to which the truly religious might penetrate, and remain untouched by sordid custom which infused the common practice of the cult. Scholars like Jane Harrison and Charles Seltman among modern writers have found a fascination in the theme, and have praised, and condoned in their description ancient practices of the mystery cults, which, to less philosophic minds, can only appear base and horrible.

Perhaps the Nicolaitans had some such preoccupations. Perhaps, too, they were those who saw in the Caesar-cult only a harmless ritual of loyalty, and not an issue of man-worship on which a Christian need stake life and livelihood. Ephesus, at any rate, taught by two apostles, had rejected such compromise. On the other hand, the hot-house intellectual life which was inseparable from Ionian Greece, first seed-bed of Greek thought, had produced its crop of false teachers, even as Paul had foreseen, and the glow of its first enthusiasm had cooled in the Christian community. It is the fashion of a church, as Ramsay brilliantly demonstrated, to interpret in its attitudes the defects and the qualities of the society in which it functions, and Ephesus, old in history, past its glory, and economically stagnant, was weary. A new infusion of life was needed. Hence the imagery, always relevant in these cryptic letters, and related to history and geography. Many of the coins of Ephesus show a date-palm, sacred to Artemis, and symbol of her life and beneficient activity. 'I will give him', writes John, 'to eat of the tree of life'.

For the church it was not to be. Ignatius, writing a generation later, gave the church high praise. It became the seat of a succession of Eastern bishops, and a notable council was held there in A.D. 431. But long decline began. The coast became malarial. The Turks came with ruin for Asia. The city died, and with it the church. The 'candlestick' was removed out of its place.

* * * * *

Recent excavation has given a clearer view of the magnificence of Ephesus, and has made it clear that the adornment of the city continued beyond its usefulness as a port. Ramsay dated the decay of Ephesus too early. Under Claudius, in the middle of the first century, and again under Trajan, at the beginning of the second century, the great theatre was remodelled. Under Claudius the monumental Marble Street was rebuilt. Nero gave a stadium, and an inscription listing the prizes has been found. Later the place was a gladiatorial arena. The shops of the silversmiths have recently been identified. It is possible to-day, as never before, to savour the Ephesus of Paul.

Such was Ephesus' prestige that adornment continued almost up to the days of the great Gothic raid in A.D. 263. Domitian, for example, was emperor, when the great boulevard which ran from the theatre to the harbour was widened and beautified to Parisian proportions. That was a generation after Paul. But the story of archaeology extends beyond the first century which is the present concern. Suffice it to say that Paul's unerring eye had again picked one of the strategic centres of the Mediterranean.

Thirteen

Joppa, Port of the Maccabees

JOPPA appears briefly in the pages of the New Testament as the scene of Peter's historic meeting with the centurion from Caesarea. Christianity followed the trade-routes, and with the scattering of the Jerusalem church Christians had taken the road to Jerusalem's port, settled at Lod, or Lydda, on the edge of Palestine's maritime plain, and eleven miles further on at the seaport itself. It was to confirm these emigrant communities in the faith that the apostle had taken his journey into the old land of the Philistines.

The Philistines, settlers, it appears, from Crete, had occupied the narrow rim of Palestine's coastal strip since the days of Abraham. Mightily reinforced in the eleventh century before Christ as a result of the great folk movements of the time, the Philistines had pressed hard upon the Hebrew people of the hills and the hinterland, aided by their iron against the Hebrew bronze. It was in fact, a confrontation of East and West. The dynamic people from the desert were infiltrating Palestine from the hills. Opposing them was a colony of Europe, for, if ethnography is read aright, and the Philistines were indeed a people from Crete, they were of Indo-European stock, a far ripple of the flood which was populating Europe, from the ancient human reservoirs of the steppes.

For all their temporary success in the days of Saul, a success which dwindled when the Hebrew enemy armed his natural zeal with iron after the conquest of Edom, the Philistines never occupied effectively any depth of country. Their earliest colony was confined to the southern portion known to-day as the Gaza Strip. Joppa lay where the maritime lowlands narrow to a spear-point of sand and plain, and no one can say whether it was a Philistine port. In all likelihood it was, for the colonists of the coast were seafarers, and a few off-shore reefs at Joppa provided such haven for ships as that wind and surf-swept coast could offer.

Joppa was a walled town in the time of Thutmosis III, in the fifteenth century. The name appears in the Pharaoh's tribute-lists. It is also mentioned in the Amarna letters, that amazing collection of correspondence from the foreign office of Amenhotep IV, which throws such vivid light on the decay of Egyptian power in Palestine before the Hebrew invasion. In the Old Testament it finds mention only three times. In 2 Chron. 2. 16 Hiram of Tyre undertakes to cut cedar in Lebanon and raft it down to Joppa. The haulage up the thirty-five miles of arduous road to Jerusalem was to be Solomon's concern. In Ezra 3. 7 a similar arrangement, almost five centuries later, is recorded. And it was at Joppa that Jonah found a ship to sail in when he fled from the task which he disliked.

For all that Joppa was part of Israel's claim. 'To the great sea, toward the going down of the sun', the land was to extend. Dan was to hold the coast at this point. The inheritance was never claimed before the Exile. Hence the rapture of the Jews when the Maccabees occupied the port and 'cleansed' it in the forties of the second century before Christ. Hence, too, the rabid nationalism which became a feature of the place, and led Herod, as will later be shown, to build afresh, free from Hebrew contamination, the port of Caesarea, thirty or more miles up the coast, in spite of the fact that Augustus had recently made Joppa and its coast a part of the royal domains. Today the old port merges geographically with the dynamic Tel Aviv, its crumbling buildings and narrow old streets in strong contrast with the modern waterfront of the bustling Hebrew city.

It is easy to imagine Peter's preoccupations as he moved about in Joppa, and visited the little community of Christians. The tradition of the town was one of Jewish pride and intransigeance. In the days of Judaean power dire things had been done in Joppa to Greeks and other Gentiles. It must have been as difficult there as in the city of Jerusalem to see the Church as something apart from Judaism, and a global community without distinction of race or caste in its membership. The narrow streets and jetties were thronged with sailormen from Greece, Italy, Phoenicia, and the cosmopolitan crowd must have stirred disturbing thoughts in the mind of a man who was moving towards a strange new liberalism.

It was surely a sign of changing outlook that he found lodging with Simon the tanner, the follower of a trade which can have left small opportunity for the ritual cleanliness beloved of the stricter Jerusalem Jews. The kindly host rigged a tarpaulin on the roof made of skins of beasts. Part of his trade was probably the manufacture of leather sails and hatch-covers for the ships of the port. Drowsy under the hanging awning, Peter fell asleep, and dreamed of a great canvas let down from heaven by its four corners filled with all manner of beasts, clean and unclean. The imagery of his dream was the last sight which fell upon his waking eyes.

It was an historic moment when the messengers from the garrison-town knocked at the door. Luke makes the most of the story, for he was determined that Paul's liberalism should be traced to its real origin, not in the bold action of the converted Pharisee, but to the constraint of the Galilæan apostle. Hence the elaboration of the account which showed the door opening to the Gentiles, not first in central Asia Minor, but a few miles from Jerusalem in nationalistic Joppa, and Herodian Caesarea.

Faith had confronted faith before on the northern Philistine coast, and Sir George Adam Smith, the geographer of Palestine, analyses a curious complex of legend which links Joppa and Lydda. It was at Joppa that Perseus, the Greek hero, rescued the maid Andromeda, chained to a rock to feed a monster of the sea. He slew the dragon and saved the girl. Curiously enough, Saint George, about whom a similar tale is told, is the patron saint of Lydda, as well as of England. According to one story he was martyred there. In any case Lydda received relics of the saint, and over many centuries pilgrims visited his alleged tomb there. A monastery was dedicated to him in the early days of monasticism, and a church bore his name. The Crusaders built a cathedral over the tomb. Saladin destroyed it, and Richard Lion-heart, who did more than most monarchs to popularise George as an English saint, built it again. Or so, at least, it is said, though sceptics aver that the ruins visible to-day were those made by the iconoclastic Saladin.

Curiously enough, and in spite of Saladin's vandalism, the Moslems revere George, and a legendary detail in their mythology takes the story a step further. Dajjal, they say, the Antichrist, will be destroyed at the gates of Lydda. The tale arose from the ancient bas-relief in the Lydda church of St. George slaying the dragon. The consonants 'n' and 'l' are frequently confused. Can Dajjal be Dagon, the ancient fish-god of the Philistines, the victim of Jehovah in an ancient trial of strength? It is curious to find Dagon, Perseus slaying the sea-monster, and Saint George killing the dragon, within the space of a score of miles.

'If the derivation be correct,' writes George Adam Smith, 'then it is indeed a curious process by which the monster, symbolic of heathenism conquered by Christianity, has been evolved out of the first great rival of the God of Israel?' Speaking of Lydda, Joppa's neighbour, he continues: 'And could there be a fitter scene for such a legend than the town where Hebrew touched Philistine, Jew struggled with Greek, and Christendom contended with Islam?'

Fourteen

Caesarea, Garrison City of Rome

THE port of Caesarea, to which Paul came under escort from Jerusalem, was a brand-new foundation, and unlike any other city in Palestine. It lay on the coast sixty-five miles from Jerusalem, designed rather to serve Samaria, which Herod had restored under the loyal name of Sebaste, then the ancient capital of Judaea. Sebaste is a title built on the Greek for Augustus, and both Caesarea and Sebaste honoured the amazing diplomat who became the first emperor of Rome, Caesar Augustus. Both names reflect the canny pro-Roman policy of the able line of Idumaean kings who served Rome in Palestine over the reigns of six emperors.

Herod held great fortresses to the east of the land appropriate to his Edomite origin. Politically, he needed a window to the west, and Rome needed entrance there. Caesarea served both. The great artificial port was a symbol of Herod's partnership with Rome.The equally remarkable building project which crowned Jerusalem with its temple, symbolised his conciliation of the Jews. The integration of the two policies was Herod's life-long preoccupation.

Rome's bridgehead was necessarily a port, and ports are difficult to find on Palestine's open surf-swept coast. The long plain which fronts the Mediterranean, from the Egyptian border to Carmel, contains no river-beds, or coastward-bent highlands which break the beach-line on more rugged shores to form harbour and haven. Hence long open roadsteads backed by sand-dunes, which offered no anchorage for ships.

Joppa was the one possible port equipped with natural protection. The place fell into Jewish hands in the time of Simon Maccabaeus at the end of the second century before Christ, and under that dynamic fanatic it was the custom to purge an occupied town of the heathen and their idols settling it with 'such men as would keep the Law'. In a seaport it must have been peculiarly difficult to put down the Greek and Phoenician maritime population on whom the functioning of the town depended. Hence half a century of faction, sedition, and strife, with occupation and reoccupation by Syrian and Jew, which left a mark on Joppa.

Pompey, the Roman, came in 63 B.C., and his able organisation of the Middle East brought order out of international chaos, and gave Palestine her first elusive taste of the Roman Peace. Part of the settlement was that Joppa became a free town. But not for long. Rome fell into civil war, as Pompey and Julius Caesar strove for supremacy, and in 47 B.C., Caesar, victorious over the Senate and his rival, gave Joppa back to the Jews. Later Augustus, the final founder of the Roman Peace, added the port to Herod's domains. It was therefore in Herod's hands to build Joppa into his Roman port.

Herod knew his Jewish subjects too well to make such a mistake. History had entered into Joppa's soul. Joppa was as violently Jewish as Jerusalem, and rabidly anti-Roman. Both Herod and the Romans knew the peril of a violent deliberate challenge to the Jews. When the Great Rebellion began in A.D. 66, Joppa was the first objective of attack when Cestius Gallus marched on Jerusalem. For a Roman beach-head Herod needed safer, less encumbered ground. It was worth the vast expense to begin from the foundations and build a new port.

Hence Caesarea. The new port bore no burden of history. Herod himself was safe there as he might scarcely have been in nationalistic Joppa. The Romans too were without the embarrassments which rendered their administration difficult in Jerusalem. Herod would view with equanimity the fact that Caesarea must have gone far to ruin Joppa's trade. Its artificial harbour was incomparably better. Its construction, in fact, was a magnificent feat of engineering. So was the city which it immediately served, and which took twelve full years to build, a city on the Greek and Roman model, with great places of popular assembly, an amphitheatre with a prospect to the sea, a temple to Rome and Augustus, a hippodrome or racecourse, and a drainage system which speaks of Roman engineers. No Jew could be at home there. The hand of the alien was in every stone and street. Crusader defence works are the most prominent feature of the surviving remains, but enough of Herod's Roman town and port survives to give a clear impression of the strength and importance of the invaluable bridgehead with which the king provided his masters.

The harbour itself was the greatest work of all. A breakwater two hundred feet wide was built against the southern gales and waves. It ran through twenty fathoms of water, and was built by dropping enormous blocks of lime-stone into the water. Some of them are said to be of the almost incredible size of fifty feet by ten by nine. To shift and so place them would tax all the resources of modern engineering. No doubt Herod had some thought in mind of rivalling his friend Agrippa, minister of Augustus, who had built a great artificial haven in Italy. The vast stones formed a mole and a quay. It was furnished with towers, and at the landward end stood a complex of warehouses. The mole, said Josephus, 'was a most pleasant place to walk for such as had a mind for exercise'. The enclosed haven was of greater area than Athens' Peiraeus. Its opening, like that of the modern Haifa, is to the north, the quarter from which the winds blow most gently.

The coastline has changed over the centuries, and the mole to-day is one hundred and sixty yards from the shore. But the harbour in its glory dwarfed the town itself, and a coin of Nero bears the inscription 'Caesarea by Augustus' Harbour'. On a coast so unprotected a good port could not be other than successful. The Roman garrison, 3,000 strong, had its headquarters there. Cornelius, who sought Peter at Joppa, was the commanding officer of a select company in the force, and himself typical of the fine officers Rome habitually chose for the difficult military assignment in her most turbulent province. 'Caesarea', said Tacitus, 'is the capital of Judaea', and so it appeared to a Roman. Amid the peril and turmoil of Palestine, Caesarea was secure and undisturbed. Here the last of the Herods, the best character of them all, Agrippa II, found refuge, and watched the ruin of his country, when the storm of the Great Rebellion raged over the land. Here Paul was safe over two years, while the slow processes of justice under two procurators of Judæa, worked themselves towards legal conclusion.

Paul had been in Caesarea under happier circumstances. He had called on his way to Jerusalem and the disastrous events which had ended his liberty. He stayed with Philip, who appears to have lived in the Gentile town for twenty years, demonstrating in the fact the completeness of the adjustment to an alien environment which marked the more enlightened of the Hellenistic Jews. Philip's first activities in the Church are described earlier in the *Acts of the Apostles*. He disappears from the record as the figure of Peter, and then of Paul, assume prominence, but his work, no doubt, went on.

And that work must have influenced the noble soldier Cornelius. Hence the story of Peter's journey from Joppa.

Events had conditioned the apostle for the task. He lodged in the house of Simon the tanner on the occasion of his visit, sleeping in the sultry afternoon on his host's flat roof with a leather awning over his head. Out of the awning, as the last chapter suggested, and Peter's own drowsy musings on the strange events which had made him disregard the ritual 'uncleanness' of the tanner's trade, was built the imagery of the vivid dream. The dream, linked by circumstance to the visit of the envoys from Caesarea, took Peter to the garrison town and the remarkable experience on which Luke set such importance. Indeed, as he wrote his account, perhaps in Caesarea while Paul was under detention, he saw the vital link between Peter and Paul, and the root and origin of all Paul's global mission in the conversion of the centurion of Caesarea.

He found the events of Paul's examination before Felix, Festus, and the visiting vassal king equally significant. He lavished his narrator's art on the account, and produced a long summary of Paul's able addresses, repetitive though some of the material is. Luke's aim was to establish the fact that responsible and informed tribunals had conceded that the new faith was not seditious, and that no law was contravened by its preaching. He sought to vindicate his friend before the Jews, and before the Romans. Hence the large proportion of his book devoted to events which took place in Herod's town.

After Roman times Caesarea fell into decay. The blight of the Arab fell upon the coast, and the Crusaders were the only intruders to give some attention to the restoration of the haven. At the end of the last century the ruins were more extensive than they are to-day, for destruction has proceeded apace in the last seventy or eighty years. All that is ended. Modern Israel, conscious of its nationhood, has a care for monuments of the historic past, and Caesarea is receiving the archaeologists' attentions. The harbour works have been surveyed by skin-divers, and interesting information gained. The theatre is under excavation, and one surprising find has been the name of Pontius Pilate in a fragmentary inscription. The garrison town, of course, was his headquarters as procurator, and the scene of a famous contest between him and a Jewish deputation in Jerusalem. Obstinate and overbearing, Pilate had hung votive shields in Herod's palace, dedicated to the Emperor. The Jews won their point by a deputation to Tiberius, and Pilate's symbols of his clumsy loyalty were transferred to Rome's shrine in Caesarea.

More will emerge as the buried remnants of the city are uncovered. They are not hidden like the relics of so many ancient towns under the accumulated buildings of the ages. Caesarea is a barren site, and open ground for the excavator. A city so typical of the three worlds which clashed and fused in Palestine, and produced the New Testament as their common document, should yield much of interest and illustration of the world of Christ and Paul.

Fifteen

Jerusalem, Sanctuary of Judaism

JERUSALEM dominates both Testaments as no other city of the Bible. It first appears as Salem, the city of the strange, good king Melchisedek, to whom the great Abraham himself gave tithes of his battle-spoil, and personal obeisance. This was twenty centuries before the Christian era, and indeed pottery fragments from before that time attest the human occupation of the site. When the city next appears in history, it is a Canaanitish stronghold, bearing allegiance to Egypt. The great Pharaoh, Thutmosis III, had made Palestine a buffer state, a pre-occupation of Egypt as old and as new as history, and the petty kings of the towns and fortresses of Palestine were charged with the task of the land's defence.

When Egypt's hands grew slack under Amenhetep IV, the royal pacifist who sought to give his land a new religion, the puppet kings of the hill-forts of Palestine found themselves menaced by nomad invaders, and presented with new problems of loyalty, expediency, and self-preservation. The story may be read in the famous Amarna letters, the collection of Amenhetep's foreign office correspondence found in the ruins of his new capital by the Nile in 1887. Some of the letters are over the signature of Abdikhiba, king of Jerusalem, who protests his loyalty to Egypt, deplores royal inaction before the mounting threat of 'the Habiru', in whom some see the Hebrew infiltrators of Palestine, and describes in urgent words the growing anarchy of the land under Egyptian supineness and military incompetence. 'The whole land, my king, is going to ruin', is the refrain in the correspondence from the hill-fortress where once the calm Melchisedek had reigned. It was the first generation of the fourteenth century before Christ . . .

In point of fact, Jerusalem was not to fall to the invaders for another four hundred years. It was in 1003 B.C. when David, in the flush of his military prowess, stormed the stronghold of the Jebusites, which held the strategic plateau later to be called by his name, 'the city of David'. Jerusalem, for all that, was no place of rest for the psalmist-king, but the scene of his sad moral ruin, of palace rebellion and intrigue, of bitterness, and defeat.

It was David's brilliant, worldly son Solomon, who gave Jerusalem her Golden Age, extended walls and area, built a palace, and a temple for Jehovah. The brilliant young king spared no expense. The alliance with the Phoenicians of Tyre, which David himself had initiated, gave David's son wealth unknown before his day. The Phoenician fleets sailed out of Ezion-geber on the Gulf of Akaba, and from India, Ceylon, and Arabia Felix riches poured in for both Jerusalem and Tyre.

Solomon rafted Lebanon cedar down from Phoenicia, and dragged the great logs up thirty-five miles of unformed road to the city, which stood 2,500 feet above the level of the sea. Gold from Ophir plated the cedar beams, and Jerusalem's temple became a wonder of the little Middle Eastern world. Its fame travelled down the desert trade routes to Shabwa, and brought the queen of the far Arabian land visiting to see. Perhaps the tradition she carried back to the land of 'gold and frankincense and myrrh' was one which persisted for nine centuries, for the Magi, who came to Bethlehem, bore gifts reminiscent of Arabia's products. Perhaps they travelled up Sheba's road, drawn by an ancient story.

The centuries brought no comparable Golden Age to Jerusalem. The city bravely resisted Assyrian siege in 701 B.C. It was the famous occasion when Isaiah's dauntless spirit held the morale of the people, and when the long Siloam tunnel was cut to bring the precious water in to sustain the besieged. Its wall-cut inscription describing the feat is one of the most ancient pieces of Hebrew script. Sennacherib, the Assyrian invader, met grim disaster south of Gaza, and Jerusalem survived, only to suffer storming, fire, looting, and utter destruction under Nebuchadnezzar of Babylon a century later.

The city lay in ruins for long years, until Babylon herself met Jerusalem's fate. The Persians, who had seized Babylon's empire, favoured the Jews, and under Ezra and Nehemiah city and temple were founded again. Disaster and restoration had made the city holy. It became a symbol of Jewish destiny and the Jewish faith, recognised by friends and foes alike during the tangled history of the centuries of change and flux when Persia perished and Alexander's successor empire fell into its four parts. Palestine again played its old rôle of buffer state between the Greek kingdom of Syria, and the Greek kingdom of Egypt. Jerusalem was the heart and core of the land in the years of subjection and vassalage, and again during the brief, bold era of independence won by the brave Maccabees from a weakening Syria.

Rome came with Pompey in 65 B.C., and it was Rome's vassal-king Herod the First, who built the great temple on the ancient site, the temple which became the scene of Christ's teaching, and also of the disaster which ended Paul's Jerusalem ministry. It was a magnificent structure, of a holiness recognised uniquely by the occupying authorities, for a surviving wall-inscription speaks of the Jews' right to preserve the sanctity of the shrine's inner court against all Gentile intrusion or trespass on pain of death. The Romans, indeed, accorded a similar sanctity to the city itself. The legions, in common practice, did not carry their standards into the city. It was Pilate's folly, in scorning this compromise, which led to the first protest of the Jews against his heavy-handed rule, and initiated the series of events by which the subtle leaders of the Jews gained power over him, a situation so tragically illustrated at the time of Christ when the priests won their way.

In the crowded street outside Pilate's judgment hall, the mob, prompted by the collaborating priests, chose Barabbas and sent Jesus Christ to death on the cross. It was a significant incident. Incredible crowds thronged Jerusalem and its environs at Passover time. The atmosphere was tense and dark with nationalistic passion, and the prophet from Galilee had disappointed the hot-headed patriots by his teaching of peace and a kingdom 'not of this world'. The palm branches on the road over the Mount of Olives had been a sign of Jewish defiance rather than of religious devotion, and now the mood was changed. The harassed Roman, instinctively seeking justice, sought to save an innocent man, and earned canonisation in the Ethiopian church by the act, but Pilate was compromised by past mistakes, and could not afford another appeal to Tiberius.

He might have known a Jerusalem mob better than to offer the alternative of Barabbas, the terrorist of the Jericho road, and the hero of the ardent nationalists for his murder of Roman soldiers. To the mob Barabbas was a man, red-blooded, real, one who faced facts, and sought the straight path to a kingdom which men could comprehend. Such a multitude was a ready tool for the hierarchy, anxious to be rid of yet another challenge to their comfort and collaborating policy. The choice revealed the spirit of the city, and it led straight to the horror, folly, and tragedy of the Great Rebellion of A.D. 66.

The siege of Jerusalem was the final and most awful episode of that conflict. Christ had foreseen its savagery when he paused on the brow of the Mount of Olives and looked down on the city beneath. The crown of the hill is higher than the eminence on which Jerusalem stands, and it was natural that the vision of the city's long troubled past, and her sombre future should break upon His mind when the road on which He journeyed topped the ridge. By the irony of fate, Titus' headquarters stood in the same place when the legions invested Jerusalem forty years later. The ridge of the Mount of Olives was a platform too for the Roman ballistas, which flung their unceasing barrage of stones and iron bolts against the walls and their defenders.

The story of the siege is one of the most awful pages of ancient history. Within the walls, amid misery, starvation, wounds, and death, faction reigned, for the curse of division and fanaticism lay on the defenders. The Romans were forced to take the city street by street, and house by house. Even then the temple resisted, and the assault troops were compelled to fight doggedly through the great complex of buildings inch by inch. Casualties were appalling, for the legions had closed in when the vast Passover crowds were in and around Jerusalem, and an appreciable proportion of the Jews of Palestine, and many visitors from Jewry overseas, lay dead in the ashes and tumbled stone which was all the Romans left behind. Hordes went into captivity, and slaved on the building of the Colosseum, the vast amphitheatre at Rome which Vespasian built for his people.

The Christians who heeded the warnings of Christ, given so insistently in the apocalyptic discourse just before He died, escaped to Pella, as the ring of Roman investment drew in round the doomed city. From this comparative safety they must have watched the fall of the Holy City. It is strange that it should even bear that name. 'Jerusalem which killeth the prophets', had been the appellation of Christ, Himself so soon to share the fate of those who had sought to speak the truth in the capital of Jewry. And Jerusalem, which rejected and crucified Christ, had also been a harsh environment for the Church which arose in His name. The stern Pharisees who formed a powerful element in its congregation, appear, in the end, to have dominated policy. Paul spent much effort in an endeavour, by monetary relief for the Jerusalem poor collected from the Gentile world, to soften and reconcile the Pharisaic wing of the Church in Jerusalem. His last perilous visit in A.D. 57 was to deliver the great gift.

There is no evidence that it was appreciated. The spirit of Jerusalem was too strong. Its very stones reeked of narrow fanaticism, of nationalistic pride, and of ancient exclusiveness. Those who formed the first ardent congregation of the Church had been scattered by the persecution of Herod Agrippa I, and the scattering was the first movement of a wider evangelism. Those who remained, or drifted back to Jerusalem when the pressure eased, were not all illiberal men, and the story of the Jerusalem Convention, which forms the centre and coping stone of the *Acts of the Apostles*, shows that it was still possible at the beginning of the ministry of Paul, to present and carry a case for a nobler and universal Christianity in the city where the faith was born.

At the end of Paul's ministry, however, the atmosphere is subtly different. Jewry the world over was slowly gathering heat against Rome. The explosion in Palestine was visibly nearer, and in the story of Paul's last visit, brilliantly told by Luke, it is possible to sense the brittle, harsh spirit of the city, and the anxiety of the Christian community not to be too obviously hostile to the entrenched forces of nationalistic Judaism. The exclusive wing was gaining control. Where was it more likely to do so . . . ?

Jerusalem rose from the ashes of A.D. 70 to die again in A.D. 132, when a second rebellion ended in the virtual destruction of Palestine. Hadrian put the Jews down at immense cost in Roman lives, smashed Jerusalem which he saw to be the centre and symbol of resistance, re-named the site after himself, and forbade Jews to live there. There was to be no more returning from exile by the willow-lined waters of another Babylon, no sending of rich tribute to a homeland destined for mystic world-wide domination, no pilgrimage to a place of sanctity and messianic promise, no sign left to remind the Empire's most intransigeant people that Rome was doomed and Jewry a chosen race. It was the opportunity of Christianity. All the shackles of Judaism were thus broken. Other heresies were to rise, but the Judaistic interpretation of the faith, which had plagued the ministry of Paul, was ended with the end of the city where it began, a city drenched with old fanaticism, fascinated by a perverse reading of its sacred book, the home and fortress of a corrupted form of a noble religion. The place was gone. The Book remained, but the Christians had made that their own.

There is none the less, a strange vitality about Jerusalem. The city rose to become a symbol of Christendom, as it had once been a symbol of Jewry. It was fought over by Saracen and Crusader. It is divided to-day between Jew and Moslem, and studded between both with the 'holy places' of the Christians. Israel, reborn and dynamic, confronts Ishmael in another Jerusalem, and for the first time in its long story it is a frontier town. All history seems to declare that such a condition of affairs cannot well endure. The tale of Jerusalem, city of Melchisedek, of David, of Christ, of Paul, of Saladin, and Allenby, had not reached its final chapter.

And when all history is done, it remains an apocalyptic type of Heaven, the 'city with foundations' of which Abraham and Plato dreamed as well as John.

Sixteen
Rome, Capital of Empire

IT was perhaps February or March in the year 59 of the first century, when Paul of Tarsus came to Rome under escort along the ancient Appian Way. It had been a hard and hazardous voyage. Caught in an autumn gale south of Crete, the corn-ship in which Paul travelled was wrecked on Malta, and it was only with the coming of spring that the apostle was able to continue his journey to Italy. He landed at Puteoli, no doubt traversed the mosquito-ridden Pontine Marshes by barge to save a night, and halted for a meal at Forum Apii, a busy little trading town, before pushing on to the village of Three Shops ten miles nearer Rome.

At both staging-posts, Christians from Rome, alerted by the little church at Puteoli, met the distinguished prisoner, and Luke reports that Paul 'took courage'. He needed such strengthening of spirit. It had been a hard and stressful winter, and a tendency to bouts of depression, according to Ramsay, is a symptom of the chronic malaria, which, if the same great scholar is correct, was Paul's 'thorn in the flesh'. Nor, indeed, was the prospect cheering as the smoke of the great city appeared ahead.

Perhaps the landscape was not very different from that which may still be seen here and there south of Rome today—hungry terrain, dark cypresses, umbrella pines, and the suggestion of age and ruin in wall, road, and garden, for Rome was already eight centuries old. The open ground outside the Capena Gate, by which Paul came in, was occupied by a Jewish shanty slum, and the sight of his poverty-stricken fellow-countrymen must have done little to lift Paul's spirits, as the centurion led his detachment into Rome. The more fortunate Jews had a ghetto across the Tiber, and it was their leaders who visited the apostle in his house-imprisonment, and ran true to the monotonous pattern of pride, prejudice, and rejection which Paul had known from Palestine to Greece.

Rome was at the height of her imperial power when Paul came to

Italy to make his appeal to Nero. It was eight hundred years since a Latin-speaking tribe who formed an enclave by the Tiber, had used one of a group of eminences on the river-bank as an acropolis. They were hemmed in by related but hostile peoples, and needed a place of refuge and defence when the raiding hillmen were abroad in the plain. The position was, in fact, ideal. The valley of the Tiber at that point is a deep trough, averaging a mile in width, cut into the soft tufa floor of the river's lower course. Ancient erosion of the edge of the trench had formed the series of hills with which the city was to be for ever associated, the Capitol, the Palatine, and the Aventine, with the Caelian, Oppian, Esquiline, Viminal and Quirinal as flat-topped spurs.

It is difficult in modern Rome to distinguish them. Twenty-seven centuries of occupation have filled valley bottoms, softened edges, removed eminences, and levelled down what must once have been a striking group of convenient hills, each, in course of time, with the growth of a peasant community, the little fort and stockade of a coherent group. The river makes a long S-shaped bend through the territory, forming in the act an island. This causes the stream to silt and shallow, and thus make the only practicable ford between the sea and the upper reaches of the watercourse. Geography thus played its rôle in history, for the occupants of the hills by the river naturally dominated the ford and the trade which passed that way, between the Etruscan north of Italy and the Greek communities of the south. Another road from the sea up the length of the Tiber valley served the hill-tribes of the hinterland.

Like Corinth, Rome thus straddled the paths of commerce, and became inevitably the magnet for immigration, and a strong outward-looking community. Archaeological evidence suggests that the hill-strongholds had coalesced to form a federation within common defences by the sixth century before Christ. Burials from the Palatine and Capitoline hills, on the edge of the marshy lowland which was to be the Forum, cease about that period, and the Cloaca Maxima, the Great Sewer, first of Rome's vast engineering works, may have been started at the same time to drain the now common territory of the federating groups.

So Rome the city began, and with it Roman history. There is a key to the understanding of that tremendous story. It is visible in the little town early in her history. Hemmed in by the powerful empire of the Etruscans to the north, by the Greek colonies to the south, and by the Oscan and Umbrian tribes of Central Italy, the Romans, as they may now be called, were forced to stand together or perish. Responding to the challenge of such encirclement, Rome thrust out and out, seeking living-space and a stable frontier. She never found one, but the out-reaching of her strength took her early to the control of Italy, and later to Northumberland, the Persian Gulf, the Rhine, the Danube, the cataracts of the Nile, and the deep Sahara.

By the fourth century before Christ, Rome was already a large and populous city. The valleys and hollows between the ancient hills formed a roading-pattern which remained throughout the city's history, and is not without traces today. By the third century the great 'islands', or tenement houses, which were to be another feature of Rome, were also visible, and suggest the overcrowding, the squalor, and the slums, which were finding presence and expression among the temples of the gods, and the mansions of senator, knight, and priest. A story of building, rebuilding, destruction, and revival, one which archaeology will never fully investigate, is written in the tangle of rubble and ruin far beneath the streets and edifices of modern Rome. The brief line of Rome's underground railway, a structure of the last generation, ran through solid ancient history.

It is possible, none the less, to piece together the record of periods of great building activity. At the end of the second century before Christ, when Rome was already penetrating the Middle East, there was a vast influx of wealth and capital from overseas provinces, and new riches were reflected in great efforts of reconstruction in the city. Pompey did much to beautify and adorn, and Augustus, first of the emperors, boasted on the temple wall of Ancyra that he 'had found the city built of brick and left it built of marble'. Augustus' bold and far-seeing attempt to bring Rome's old religion to life, itself multiplied Rome's temples, and gave a great library to the city attached to the shrine of Apollo, the youthful god whom Augustus devoutly served.

He thus set the fashion for his successors, and it is from the second century after Christ that most of Rome's surviving ruins date—the great baths of Caracalla and Diocletian, for example, and those of Constantine. Most famous of all remaining relics, the Flavian Amphitheatre, still called by its medieval name of Colosseum, was built by Vespasian, who, until his troops raised him to empire in

A.D. 69, was the commander of the Palestine legions at grips with the great Jewish rebellion.

A vivid picture of the perils and inconveniences of life in Rome at the turn of the first century after Christ, may be read in the third satire of the mordant poet Juvenal. Juvenal knew Rome from the angle of the poor and the outcast, and writes bitterly of the misery, poverty, and inhumanity of the slum-ridden city, and the cruel inequalities between its inordinately rich and its shockingly poor. The million-mark in population was probably passed at the beginning of the Christian era, and it was a motley, cosmopolitan multitude. 'The Orontes has flowed into the Tiber', wrote Juvenal in the satire quoted, and he ranks the self-seeking foreign rabble with the dangers of traffic, fire, and jerry-built houses which endangered his small world.

No one knows who first brought Christianity to Rome, but Paul found a church functioning there. It is possible that the disturbances which led Claudius to expel the Jews in A.D. 49, marked troubles in the ghetto associated with the first Christian preaching in the capital. Writing half a century later, the historian Suetonius states that the trouble was 'at the instigation of one Chrestos'. It seems that the garbled account, which confuses two Greek words 'christos' and 'chrestos', retains some recollection of Jewish tension over the new faith, and indeed of such breaches of the peace as those which Paul endured more than once in the provinces, but which were not to be tolerated in metropolitan Rome. The curious Nazareth Decree relates, no doubt, to the same incident.

Aquila and Priscilla suffered under Claudius' anti-semitic decree, but by the date of Paul's arrival both Synagogue and Church were back in Rome under another emperor, the young Nero, who initiated the policy of persecution against the Christians after the great fire of July 19, A.D. 64. Persecution was sporadic from Nero's time onward, and never destroyed the Church. It did, however, lead to the use of the catacombs as meeting and burial places, and provided thereby a method of calculating the possible number of Christians in Rome. Ten generations of Christians are buried in the catacombs, and the total of their graves would obviously give an average figure of Christians per generation. It is difficult to reach an accurate estimate of the length of the famous galleries cut in Rome's tufa base, but the lowest estimate is 350 miles, and the highest 600. The lowest estimate of the burials they contain is 1,175,000, the highest 4,000,000.

Given an average population for Rome of 1,000,000, for the ten generations involved, the figure of 175,000 per generation emerges on the lower estimate of burials, 400,000 on the higher. It is obvious that Gibbon's estimate of one twentieth for the Christian minority of Rome is quite wrong. The most conservative estimate from the indisputable evidence of the catacomb burials shows that, on an average, at least one fifth of Rome's population were Christians. There must have been times when it was a much higher proportion.

Rome, like Babylon, became an image of carnal, organised paganism. In the lurid poetry of the document of protest which closes the canon of the New Testament, empire and city are mingled as symbols of sin. Chapters 17 and 18 of the Apocalypse look grimly forward to just such a fate for Rome as Rome had wreaked on Jerusalem, on Corinth, on Carthage, and many another city of her foes, just such a fate as Rome did in fact suffer under the fire and sword of Alaric the Goth. The former oracle, passionate in its imagery, pictures Rome sitting like a woman of sin on her famous seven hills, polluting the world with her vice. The second of the two chapters, cast in the form of a Hebrew 'taunt-song', and imitating Ezekiel's chapter on Tyre, pictures the galleys loading cargo for Rome in some eastern port. There was 'merchandise of gold, and silver, and precious stones, and of pearls, and of fine linen, and purple, and silk, and scarlet, vessels of ivory, and precious wood, and of brass, and iron, and marble, cinnamon, and frankincense, beasts, and sheep, and horses, and chariots, and slaves, and the souls of men'.

The climax is shocking, as the writer pictures Ostia, the Tiber port of Rome, in the stark ruin in which, indeed, it may be seen today, its great warehouses empty shells revealed by the archaeologist's spade, its streets empty, and its courtyards desolate. Amid all the voices of praise from the first century one alone cried protest against Rome's domination of the souls of men. That voice was a Christian voice, and history took heed of it.

Paul had no such view of Rome when he rode up the long Appian Way. He still hoped that the Empire would choose Christ. The panic fear, born of the fire and the suspicion of imperial incendiarism which followed it, and which precipitated Nero's cynical persecution, was still five years away. True enough, the young ruler had already revealed his sinister nature. He had come to power aided by his mother's intrigues and crimes. That was five years earlier. And in A.D. 59, the very year of Paul's arrival, if the date is fixed aright, Nero killed his mother who had sought too characteristically to dominate him. Rome was becoming aware of the base personality of him who held power, but was to tolerate him for another ten years. The year A.D. 69 was 'the year of the four emperors', when the frontier legions learned again their power, and their varied nominees strove for supremacy in a blood-drenched Italy. 'All the world wondered after the Beast', wrote John, 'for its deadly wound was healed'. Indeed, A.D. 69 might have wounded the Empire to death, had the barbarian peoples beyond the frontier known how to aid the dagger-thrust as Nero's freedman did in A.D. 68, as the deposed prince paused on the edge of suicide.

When Paul pleaded his case he found, it seems, acquittal, for there was no crime in professing Christ. What a scene it would have been in Luke's lucid style, if indeed the case did not lapse through the defection of the accusers, or the loss of the documents on the Malta beach. But all is vague. Luke died or failed to write. It is as though Paul was lost amid the Roman throng. A few touches in the letter to Philippi tell of his high mood in trouble, and of his unceasing urgency, in all conditions, to preach, but that is all . . . There is one glimpse of a later imprisonment, perhaps in A.D. 67, when he was hustled from Troas without his cloak. Death followed, for Rome had become Rome the persecutor, hated by John, the writer of the Apocalypse, for the crimes of her persecutions. For near three centuries it was to be hard to be a Christian in Rome. The catacombs are astonishing evidence for the multitude who faced the daunting prospect, lived and died for their convictions, and left the world in debt.

Seventeen

Alexandria, Queen of Egypt

ALEXANDRIA hovers on the edge of the New Testament story, and has only a precarious place in this list of its cities. It was a ship of Alexandria which carried Paul from Myra in Lycia to the Malta beach. From Alexandria came Apollos, the Jewish scholar, whose version of the Gospel had great influence in Corinth. Apart from these brief references, the New Testament has nothing to say. But there was undoubtedly a Christian church in the great sea-port of the Nile, and its activities occasioned the first mention of Christian missionaries in the secular writing of the world. At least, so it seems, if a papyrus document of the Emperor Claudius is interpreted aright.

Alexandria, as its name records, was founded by the Greek conqueror Alexander himself. The date was 332 B.C., and the motive was clear. Alexander's small army was moving rapidly through the crumbling provinces of the sprawling Persian Empire, and communications were a matter of importance if Greece and Europe were to be held, as the Macedonian king penetrated deeper and deeper into the East. Alexandria with its large harbour facilities provided such a base. It became a seat of Greek government, replacing Egyptian Memphis, a generation later, when Ptolemy, Alexander's general, took Egypt as his share of the succession. With Ptolemy, Greek Egypt began, and lasted three centuries. Fourteen Ptolemies sat on the throne, and the last of the varied line was the famous Cleopatra who almost divided the Roman Empire.

Alexandria of the first century was a vast metropolis. With its native Egyptian proletariat, its thronging Greeks, who were its first rulers and always its intelligentsia, its Roman officials alert for the safety of a vital grain-port, its huge ghetto of clever and turbulent Jews, Alexandria housed an explosive mixture. A million people, slaves and free, must have thronged the level streets, and the problems of the multi-racial community were those of Corinth on a grander scale. In the modern world Johannesburg or Singapore might understand them.

Portent had promised such a host. Alexander's engineers were laying out the lines of the city with flour on the level sand, when hordes of sea-birds from the lagoons and papyrus marshes, swept down upon the food, fighting noisily as they pecked it away. The king was perturbed, but his soothsayers interpreted the omen as one of ebullient life and prosperity. And indeed so it was to be, together with contention, passionate politics and sedition.

Dinocrates, the engineer in charge, was a man with ideas suited to the task. He it was who proposed to carve Mount Athos into a vast statue of Alexander, holding a town in one hand and pouring a stream into the sea from the other. Alexandria was worthy of his genius. Built on a grid-pattern three miles square, the city stood on a strip of sand between Lake Mareotis and the sea, cut off significantly from Egypt proper. Offshore lay the long island of Pharos, later connected with the city by a mole, giving Alexandria an outer as well as an inner harbour.

The road out the mole must have been a favourite promenade. In the first century it must have been possible for strollers to appreciate Sostratus' posthumous joke. Sostratus of Cnidus, in the reign of Ptolemy II had built a lighthouse on Pharos, which was listed as one of the wonders of the world. The French for lighthouse is still 'phare'. It was built of white marble, tapering cube on cube to a height of 590 feet, a glittering pillar of gleaming stone by day, and by night a lofty torch sending light over thirty miles or more of sea. Ptolemy had insisted on adorning the base with an inscription eulogising himself, but Sostratus carved it in the limestone with which he sheathed the lower section. Over the years, the sea, wind, and salt spray ate the limestone away, and the Alexandrians became delightedly aware that underneath, carved into the hard marble and fresh from the chisel, was another inscription: 'Sostratus of Cnidus, to the saving gods, for navigation'.

The city was an array of palaces and public buildings unique in the world, in the midst of parks and gardens like some ancient Canberra or Washington. The royal palace occupied a whole section of the waterfront, while the temple of Serapis was one of the finest buildings in the world. The temple of Pan is described by the geographer Strabo as an artificial rock mound like a pine-cone, from the top of which was a panorama of the whole city. Ancient writers speak of other buildings too numerous to mention. Set the whole magnificent place in the midst of still blue waters and luscious green, its marble white under an Egyptian sun, fill its broad bright streets with a vivid Greek crowd, with swarthy Egyptians, and dignified Jews, crowd the harbours and canals with the galleys of the world, and the picture emerges of an ancient city more like a great modern metropolis than any other centre of the first century.

The papyri, preserved in still legible condition in the Egyptian sands, give a picture of life as it was lived by great and small in the city itself, in the green lands of the Delta, and in the little towns down the Nile Valley, also without parallel in the records of the ancient world. The Greek rulers of Egypt inherited from the Pharaohs a ruthless bureaucracy which the Old Testament story of Joseph shows briefly in efficient operation. It was system of control and taxation, hag-ridden by officials, and inevitably riddled with graft and corruption, which must have borne heavily on the little man. The documents are multitudinous, agreements, contracts, proclamations, private letters, and the thousand scraps of discarded paper which from then to now find the rubbish basket and the disposal dump.

Tax and regulation did not destroy the trade of a city so ideally placed. The intruding Parthians had endangered the trade-routes of the Asian caravans, and like the Mongols of the Middle Ages had driven commerce to the seas. The Red Sea route was never more widely used than in the first century, and from the Red Sea ships in the India trade could find their way through desert canals to the Nile and the harbours of Alexandria. Or so it seems from the scanty traces in the sand, and the absence of port-facilities on the Gulf of Suez. Larger ships plied the Mediterranean. Egypt was a great wheat-growing land vital to Rome, and under special provincial administration. Great galleys bore the cargoes, on one of which Paul sailed. It carried a cargo of wheat which was jettisoned off Malta, and 276 passengers and crew.

Alexandria of the first century was abundantly possessed of the wherewithal to fill the holds of the returning Indian fleet. In those days as now the hosts of India were great customers for textiles. The native flax of Egypt supplied a linen industry whose products have been traced as far as Britain. Then there was the world monopoly of writing materials, the products of the papyrus plant. The marshes north of the Delta were the chief home of the papyrus plant, which was used not only for the fabrication of writing materials but for various other purposes. It furnished sails for boats, it was woven into mats and sandals, and bundles of the long stems carefully fitted together served as canoes. A document dating from 5 B.C. reveals the care with which the industry was regulated. It is the text of a lease of a papyrus marsh by one Dionysia, and her son to the firm of Hierax and Papus for 3 years at 5,000 silver drachmae net a year. After a long preamble the text runs: 'It shall not be lawful for them to employ workmen under the lease, at more than the current rate of wages. They shall not use pick-axes nor gather immature plants, nor cut from boats, nor sell articles made of rushes. They shall not sublet, nor pasture cattle on the property. They shall fill, shape, and render navigable the cross-streams, at their expense, just as they have received them. If, in the event of warfare, inundation, or the government, there is interference with the work, Dionysia shall have no responsibility, and it shall not be lawful for the lessees to abandon the lease, within the period.'—and so on for another full page of script, a typical legal document. They loved to see their documents drawn up legally and in order in Alexandria. Receipts occupy two and three pages of papyrus. Here is only a part of the preamble to a will by two parents: 'Whereas we have been joined together in wedlock, affording each other no ordinary peace and comfort, soothing and comforting and serving and obeying and submitting, in no single matter disagreeing, therefore we, providing against the chance that contrary to our expectation one of us should depart this life, and the survivor should find himself reduced to want by our common children, being sane and of a clear judgment, having our understanding vigorous and our mind unimpaired, our sense sound, walking on our feet at market, come forward to make this written agreement.'

But to return to the wealth of Alexandria. Its textiles and paper were probably only a portion of the produce which left her port. There were probably re-exports of manufactured produce whose raw material was supplied by the east. Take jewellery for instance. It seems most unlikely that the pearls brought in by the dhows from the Gulf were distributed unmounted. Neither can we imagine that a city with weaving and textile resources passed on unmanufactured the silks which must have come in large quantities from the East, and the serica or Indian muslin, in which in later centuries even the common people indulged. Imagine, too, the taxable wealth of the city, the port dues of all this trade, the multitudinous exactions of fines of which the papyri speak, and the wealth of the court becomes comprehensible. There were others sources too. Monopolies, for instance, were a conspicuous feature of the fiscal policy of the Ptolemies. Of these the oil monopoly was the most important. The government exercised a strict control over every stage of the industry from the sowing of the crops to the retailing of the product. It determined the acreage to be sown each year. Its agents, in conjunction with the contractors or lessees of the monopoly, superintended the sowing and harvesting, and bought up the crop at fixed prices. The oil was then manufactured in state factories and it was sold under fixed prices and conditions. No private manufacture and no importation was permitted. The papyrus draft of the law runs into a dozen pages.

Before passing to the great Museum and its scholars, a glance through a window opened by Theocritus will be of interest. It is true that Theocritus wrote his 15th Idyll, really a little mime, 150 years before the Christian era, but the life it shows must have been much the same about the court of Cleopatra, and in the first century. Two Syracusan visitors attend the festival of Adonis at the court of Ptolemy Philadelphus. Enter Gorgo. 'Is Praxinoë at home? P. She *is*. What a stranger you are. Eunoë, put a cushion on the chair. G. It does most charmingly as it is. P. Do sit down. G. Oh I thought I should never get here. The crowd! Men in uniform everywhere. You really do live too far out. P. It is all the fault of that madman of mine. Here he comes to the ends of the world and takes a *hole*—you can't call it a house—just to keep us apart—jealous spiteful wretch. G. Hush, my *dear* girl, don't talk of your husband like that before the little boy, look how he is staring! Never mind, Zopyrion, my sweet child. Mother is not speaking about papa. Nice papa! P. Yes, that papa of his, I sent him to the shop to get some soap and rouge. He came with salt, the fool. G. Same with my fellow—he can't shop. But come, we must get to the palace. I hear Arsinoe has provided something splendid. Hurry Eunoë with the water—see how the girl carries it—look silly, you are wetting my dress. G. Praxinoë that full dress becomes you wonderfully. Tell me, how much was the material. P. Don't speak of it. Eight pounds in good silver and the *work* I put into it! G. Well it is most successful. P. Bring my hat and shawl. No child I *shall not* take you. Cry as much as you like. There are bogies, there's a horse that bites! Eunoë take him, call the dog in, shut the street door.'

They go out into the street and we get a vivid picture of the Alexandrian crowd, the fine clothes and the fine chariots. They cannot pass some embroideries on display in a shop window and stand talking about them in broad Syracusan Doric until a stranger, a testy old fellow, appeals to them to keep quiet. 'You tiresome women, for Heaven's sake, stop your endless cooing talk. You bore me to death with your eternal broad vowels.' 'Indeed' says Gorgo, looking him up and down, 'And where may this person come from who pretends to speak to ladies of Syracuse. Dorian women may lawfully speak Doric I presume!' And so on.

Alexandria is chiefly remembered for its vast contribution to learning and to literature. Ptolemy I founded a vast library at Alexandria and a 'museum'. The word bears no relation to its modern sense. The Alexandrian Museum was a research institute housing a hundred scholars drawn from all parts of the Mediterranean world. Round both library and institute a cultured society collected, and a Silver Age of Greek literature dawned from which Latin literature derived deep stimulus and inspiration. The library, the 'hen-coop of the Muses' as an Athenian unkindly called it, was a magnificent collection on which the cultured court had spent much money and not a little guile. Ptolemy II borrowed the state copy of the tragedians from Athens. He left huge security, something like £50,000 in modern currency. What was £50,000 to Ptolemy? He had a copy deluxe of the tragedians made, and sent it to Athens with his compliments, surrendering his security money. The volume itself stayed in Alexandria.

It was on the advice of Demetrius of Phaleron, when, driven from Athens, he took refuge with Ptolemy I, that the prince founded the library. One of the functions of the head of the library became the educating of the royal children and so it came about that a very real university began in Alexandria. Scholars gathered round the growing collection of books and a real literature grew up. The immense task of cataloguing, first entrusted to Callimachus, suggested methods of classification, and made the Alexandrian scholars pioneers of historical and literary criticism and lexicography. But the Alexandrians are not to be lightly dismissed as pedants. It is true that there is a rather self-conscious scholarship in much of their work; it is true that their art is sometimes too apparent, but it is also true that they bridge the gap between Greece and Rome, and that, but for them, Greek poetry might have perished out of the earth, and Latin poetry might never have been born. Their poetry has been called artificial. All poetry has artifice, and in Alexandria the French critic Taine could find much to support his climatic theories of literature. The town was and is an artificial one. Its very trees were man-made groves, its flowers were in garden beds, its grass was lawn. No mountains cut its sky. The sea alone was nature undefiled. It is to the Alexandrians' credit that in a post-classical age they dedicated their efforts to the production of new and minor forms and to the task, which, by the first century B.C., had become their pre-occupation, the preservation and interpretation of the classics. We peer in vain into the past to gain some idea of life as it was lived among Alexandria's books and scholarship. Did rhapsodists, in Cleopatra's day, still chant Homer? Was Menander played, and Sappho sung? Did eager youths dispute around some later Socrates? Were lectures given by the lexicographers on that creation of Alexandria, the science of textual criticism? Who read the many books, and when and how? Where were the schools for which the many classified reading lists which have come down to us were prepared? Did Alexandria's scholars still dispute by mail with Pergamum and Rhodes? We must be content to ask the question and imagine ripe scholarship, rich in the possessions of the past, rich in its own considerable tradition, living honoured in a brilliant community.

No account of Alexandria can omit mention of the powerful Jewish community. The great pogrom of A.D. 42, the occasion of Claudius' famous document detailing his religious policy, has focussed a good deal of attention on the ancient people and the problems they occasioned. In Alexandria the largest and most troublesome section of the Jewish dispersion lived side by side with the most unruly riffraff of the Greeks. Their community claimed to be coeval with the city itself. It had received special concessions either from Alexander or the first of the Ptolemies. They rapidly overflowed the North Eastern quarter, their statutory ghetto, and when, in A.D. 42, the bungling Flaccus declared foreigners and aliens all Jews in the Greek quarters of the city, no fewer than 400 houses and business establishments were destroyed by the mob. What were they doing? We may reasonably suppose that their presence was not unconnected with Alexandria's foreign trade. A close corporation, ruled by their own senate, they must have had all that cohesion which makes the power of the modern trust and the hatred they inspired was not all nationalistic.

Two matters in the same connection must be mentioned in conclusion. The first is the great literary achievement of the Septuagint. This Greek version of the Old Testament was a response to the literary preoccupations of Alexandria. Determined to show the cultural worth of their own heritage, the Jews produced the famous translation in the middle of the third century before Christ. Legends surround its origin, and it is not impossible that the initiative did come, as one story insists, from the library itself. It is more probable that Jewish national consciousness, together with the need to provide an intelligible Bible for a host of proselytes and Gentile adherents in the synagogue, suggested the project. Historically it was of vast importance, and the fact that the quotations of the Old Testament come from this version, is indication enough of its influence and popularity.

It was probably from the Synagogue that the first Christian community came. Its link with the New Testament is through Apollos, the friend of Aquila and Priscilla. It seems also to have occasioned the first reference in secular literature to Christian missionaries. Shocking riots in Alexandria had marked the end of the reign of the mad Caligula. Flaccus, governor of Egypt, taking the hint from Rome and the young emperor's anti-Semitism, had provoked a pogrom which almost exploded into civil war. It is quite certain that only the timely assassination of Caligula prevented a Jewish war thirty years before the tragic Great Rebellion. The learned Claudius, already in middle age, succeeded to the principate, and brought to bear upon the Alexandrian question his deep knowledge of the religions of the Empire. In a papyrus document which has survived he deals in his usual wordy fashion with the troubles of the turbulent Egyptian city, and concludes his long letter with this paragraph:

> 'As for the question which party was responsible for the riots and feud (or rather, if the truth must be told, the war) with the Jews, although in confrontation with their opponents, your ambassadors, and particularly Dionysius, son of Theon, contended with great zeal; nevertheless, I was unwilling to make a strict inquiry, though guarding within me a store of immutable indignation against whichever party renews the conflict; and I tell you once for all that unless you put a stop to this ruinous and obstinate enmity against each other, I shall be driven to show what a benevolent prince can be when turned to righteous indignation. Wherefore once again I conjure you that on the one hand the Alexandrians show themselves forbearing and kindly towards the Jews who for many years have dwelt in the same city, and

dishonour none of the rites observed by them in the worship of their god, but allow them to observe their customs as in the time of the deified Augustus, which customs Augustus, which customs I also, after hearing both sides, have sanctioned; and on the other hand I explicitly order the Jews not to agitate for more privileges than they formerly possessed, and not in future to send out a separate embassy as if they lived in a separate city, a thing unprecedented, and not to force their way into gymnasiarchic or cosmetic games, while enjoying their own privileges and sharing a great abundance of advantages in a city not their own, and not to bring in or admit Jews who come down the river from Syria or Egypt, a proceeding which will compel me to conceive serious suspicions; otherwise I will by all means take vengeance on them as fomenters of what is a general plague infecting the whole world. If desisting from these courses you consent to live with mutual forbearance and kindliness, I on my side will exercise a solicitude of very long standing for the city, as one which is bound to us by traditional friendship. I bear witness to my friend Barbillus of the solicitude which he has always shown for you in my presence and of the extreme zeal with which he has now advocated your cause, and likewise to my friend Tiberius Claudius Archibius. Farewell.'

Were 'the Jews who came down the river' the first envoys of the Church? And what was its colouring? It may be guessed that it was Hebrew rather than Greek, for Apollos had to be instructed in Pauline doctrine, and Alexandria became the home of strange allegorical interpretations of the Old Testament, quite alien to Paul's Hellenistic approach. For example the Epistle of Barnabas, an Alexandrian Christian document of early date, argues from Genesis 14. 14 and 18. 23 that Abraham had a household of 318 people. The Greek for 18 is iota followed by eta, and these two letters happen to be the first two letters of 'Jesus' spelt in Greek. The Greek for 300 is tau which letter is shaped like a capital T. This is probably what the cross on which Christ was crucified looked like, rather than its traditional form with the upward projection. The cross-beam was carried by the victim, and pegged on a permanent upright. Hence the cry, 'Crucify Him', which literally says, 'Stake Him'. Arguing from these irrelevant facts some Alexandrian saw in the numerical strength of the household of Abraham a prophecy of the Christ crucified. Perhaps Apollos needed very much reorientation before he could be useful in the Greek world. With his character sketch in Acts 18. 24 we can leave Alexandria.

Eighteen

Smyrna, Ally of Rome

TO pass from the cities of Paul to the cities of John is to move into another world. A generation or more has passed into history, if the last book of the Bible was indeed written by John, the apostle, in Domitian's day. The most ancient tradition of the Church regards the political prisoner on Patmos as no other than the bishop of the Asian churches, last survivor of the Twelve, John, the intimate of Christ. The date must have been about A.D. 85. The cities of Paul are cities of the fifth and sixth decades, sharply clear in Luke's plain language. The cities of John are cities of the eighth and ninth decades of the century, seen 'as through a glass darkly', behind the obscure apocalyptic language of the prisoner, who sought to screen his meaning from hostile and uninitiated eyes.

The picture is clear for the perceptive who can read the truth behind the imagery. Sir William Ramsay, to whose archaeological work the reader of the New Testament must be forever indebted, has demonstrated this fact strikingly. Apocalyptic writing is a branch of prose-poetry, difficult to understand because the key to the imagery is so often not readily at hand. It is none the less not 'private imagery', of the sort that so often renders modern poetry obscure. Those who were meant to comprehend caught the meaning of reference and allusion, and saw plainly enough the message of the writer. For Asian Christians, *Revelation* was a more meaningful piece of writing than T. S. Eliot's *Waste Land* would be to the average church community today. Ramsay showed, in the case of the seven letters which fill the second and third chapters of the book, that much of the imagery has direct reference and application to geographical, historical, and social features familiar to readers in the seven congregations to which the cryptic letters were sent.

In the same demonstration Ramsay also developed the thesis that the Christian community in each case to some extent reflected the faults and excellencies of the city in which it found its domicile.

Ephesus, where the tracks of Paul and John crossed, is a convincing example. The city occupies a large place in first-century church history. It was the scene of a ministry described at length in Luke's narrative, and a recipient of warning on the Miletus beach. Paul's letter, written five years later, throws strong light on the solidity of the foundation which the writer laid. And then, thirty years later still, there appears in John's letter the Ephesian church of the eighties, weary but faithful, lacking somewhat in ardour, continuing, but in danger of decay. It was the living picture of the city at large, past its splendour, backward-looking, and in fear of final decadence.

Smyrna is as luminous an illustration of Ramsay's thesis. The city lies at the head of the gulf into which the Hermus empties its waters, a well-protected harbour, and the natural terminal of a great inland trade-route up the Hermus valley. The old Greek colonists had a good eye for position, and Aeolian Greeks were the first settlers on the site, a trading-post, no doubt, which was early overlaid by Ionian Greeks. All this was in the dim centuries while the Aegean world still lay in the shadow of the dark age which had followed the southward movement of yet another ripple of invasion, the coming of the Dorian Greeks.

When history takes more certain shape, as the little central Mediterranean world emerged from the centuries of breakdown, Smyrna was already a sturdy community, able and ready to do battle with the Lydian power of Sardis. Mimnermus, the poet of Smyrna of the seventh century before Christ, mentions such strife in the Hermus valley. It ended in catastrophe about 600 B.C., when Alyattes of Lydia captured Smyrna and wrecked it. For four centuries history paused. Clusters of Lydian villages occupied the site and the shoreline of the gulf, but the Greek city lay dead over the middle centuries of the millennium before Christ. That is why the writer of the letter opens with the phrase: 'These things says the first and the last, who died and came to life'. The Greek phrase used here for 'died' is literally 'became a corpse'.

That is precisely what happened to the Greek community on the gulf . . . It likewise rose from the dead. To refound Smyrna was a project of Alexander the Great, but it was not carried into effect until the days of Lysimachus, who ruled Thrace and N.W. Asia Minor in the divided empire which followed Alexander's sudden and untimely death. In 290 B.C. Smyrna was again a Greek city, with assembly and magistrates, free, and proud. From this point on, the superb commercial site ensured prosperity and lasting vitality. In Asiatic Turkey today, Izmir is one of the strongest and most dynamic communities. So decisive is geography. Shrewd policy also aided. Smyrna, in fact, owed much of her success to an early and swift appraisal of the rising power of Rome. A common peril had united the virile Italian republic with the Asian Hellenic city as early as the end of the third century before Christ. Antiochus the Great of Syria was a danger to both states, and firm alliance was an advantage to both. Smyrna was an ideal bridgehead for those whose destiny pointed to the east, and she provided at the same time a useful counterpoise in the middle Mediterranean to the naval power of Rhodes.

It was to this faithful alliance that the Smyrnaeans referred in A.D. 26 when they petitioned the emperor Tiberius to grant them permission to build a temple to his deity. Tacitus tells the story. 'The Smyrnaeans', he wrote, 'having appealed to their ancient records to show whether Tantalus, the son of Jupiter, or Theseus, the son also of a god, or one of the Amazons was their founder, proceeded to the considerations in which they chiefly trusted, namely, their friendly services to the Roman people. They had aided Rome with a naval force, they said, not only in their wars abroad, but also in those they had fought in Italy. It was they, they said, who had first reared a temple in honour of Rome, when the power of the Roman people, though great, had not yet reached its highest glory, for the city of Carthage still stood, and powerful kings governed Asia. Sulla, too, they said, had experienced their generosity, when his army was in imminent peril from the bitter weather and scarcity of clothes. When the matter was made known in the citizens' assembly at Smyrna, all present stripped off their garments and sent them to the legions'.

Of the eleven applicants, Smyrna was in consequence preferred, and became the site for the second Asian temple to the deity of Rome and the emperor, and the seat of the sinister Caesar-cult which was to cause so much suffering in the Church. To some such revival of persecution the letter refers. They were to endure tribulation 'for ten days' and some were 'to be cast into prison'. Ten days signifies a fixed period. Prison was the prelude to exile or death. At Smyrna as elsewhere the imperial policy of suppression was carried out sporadically, and Domitian, no doubt, was the cause of this outburst with the help of a hostile synagogue, against whose machinations the letter has a scornful word to say. With legislation on the books against the

Church, as it had been since the middle sixties of the century, such situations as those which Paul had found frustrating and damaging in an earlier decade, assumed a new possibility of menace and danger. Smyrna had worshipped the spirit of Rome since 195 B.C. The temple to Tiberius increased the pride she held in this historic rôle. To abstain in Smyrna was probably more serious than in Ephesus and elsewhere, more readily observed, and more diligently punished.

Hence the exhortation in the letter to endure, and win 'the crown of life'. The phrase illustrates Sir William Ramsay's point about the imagery of the communication. Smyrna was overtopped by a hill which juts towards the sea from the Asian plateau. It was a handsome city, and the buildings climbed the hill-slopes and topped its summit like a splendid crown. Hence a traditional compliment. Apollonius of Tyana mentions the feature. He wrote: 'For though your city is the most beautiful of all cities under the sun, and makes the sea its own, and holds the fountains of Zephyrus, yet it is a greater charm to wear a crown of men than a crown of porticoes, for buildings are seen only in their one place, but men are seen everywhere, and spoken about everywhere, and make their city as vast as the range of countries which they visit.'

Aelius Aristides, who knew Smyrna well, spoke in similar terms. He compares the city to the crown of Ariadne, shining in the heavens. He describes it as a statue with its feet in the sea, and rising to its crowned head at the hill-top. Apollonius wrote about the time John's letter was written. He, like the writer, was in peril under Domitian. Aristides wrote half a century or more later. Both writers show that 'the crown of Smyrna' was a recognised image of rhetoric. The Christians of Smyrna are bidden look beyond it to a greater crown. John is sure that they will so look, and, in the inspiration of the thought, endure.

Polycarp, who became Smyrna's greatest martyr and bishop, was living at the time the letter was written on Patmos. He was over ninety years of age when he died in A.D. 155, and formed a link between the apostles and the second century. The proconsul, runs the story, urged him to deny his faith and save his life. 'Swear, and I will set you free', he said. 'Reproach Christ'. The old man answered: 'Eighty and six years have I served Him, and He never did me any wrong. How then can I blaspheme my King and Saviour?' The action of the synagogue on that occasion throws light upon the letter written seventy years before. The eagerness of the Jews to expedite the execution of the aged bishop overcame their sabbatarian scruples. They came into the gay assemblage in the stadium bearing faggots for the fire. The games had ended in the late morning, the trial was then held, and in the afternoon Polycarp died. Like those who demanded the death of Christ, but refused to tread on Pilate's floor, the Jews of Smyrna may have retained ritual cleanliness by avoiding attendance at the games. Hearing the glad news of their enemy's condemnation, they may have dedicated the afternoon to the eminently religious occupation of destroying a rebel against Judaism. The rabid opposition which Paul encountered in the cities of Greece and Asia, and in Jerusalem itself, was evidently as virulent after Hadrian's destruction of metropolitan Jewry in A.D. 132 as it had been before the first rebellion.

When Christianity first came to Smyrna is not known. The guild-master's speech at Ephesus complained that the subversive activities of the Christians had infected all Asia. Perhaps the foundations for the Christian communities of Asia were indeed laid during Paul's ministry. John certainly built diligently upon them. Of all the cities in his pastoral care, Smyrna wins his most unstinted admiration. It was well-earned. Smyrna's Christians stood well in the first century. They continued to stand, and Smyrna was one of the Asian cities which withstood the Turk, and was among the last to fall to Islam. Such resistance played a salutary part in history. The delaying action of surviving remnants of the Roman Empire in the east allowed Europe time to emerge from the torpor of the Middle Ages, and receive with creative and more appreciative hands those gifts which brought the Renaissance to birth.

Nineteen

Pergamum, Cathedral City of the Imperial Cult

FIFTEEN miles from the sea, with the hills round Smyrna and the blue line of Lesbos in fine distant view, a great humped hill rises to dominate the broad Caicus plain. This royal eminence formed Pergamum's first acropolis. The foundation of the city goes back to the beginnings of urban life in Asia, but little is known of the first centuries. Coinage, with which Pergamum emerges into history, goes back to the fifth century before Christ. The city's royal estate goes back to the year 282 B.C., when Philetaerus threw off allegiance to Lysimachus, who ruled the land after the break-up of Alexander's empire.

The kingdom of Pergamum thus founded endured until 133 B.C., almost exactly a century and a half. Over this time the frontiers advanced or retreated as the power of the greater rival successor-state, Syria, ebbed or flowed. When Rome was forced to intervene in Asia Minor, to protect her eastern flank from the dynamic imperialism of Antiochus of Syria, Pergamum was a useful ally, and an equally useful buffer state, when Antiochus was decisively checked in 190 B.C. It was then that Pergamum reached its highest point of power.

Like Smyrna, Pergamum read well the signs of history, and when Attalus III bequeathed the kingdom to Rome in 133 B.C., the legacy was no doubt approved by his people, who saw little future for liberty and independence in the growing chaos of the Middle East. It was shrewd policy to seek early protection, as the Mediterranean world moved obviously nearer to an era of great rivalries and power politics on a far grander scale than the centuries of the city-states had known. Rome, in such peril, was the better wager. The Republic saw the advantage of a bridgehead so broad beyond the Aegean, accepted the royal bequest, and organised the kingdom of Pergamum into the Province of Asia. For another two and a half centuries, Pergamum remained Rome's official centre in the province. The city was therefore a seat of sovereign government for four full centuries.

Over a period of almost ninety years Pergamum has been extensively and expertly excavated and it is possible to gain a better picture of the city, with its sweep of temples and public buildings crowned by the great altar to Zeus, than of any other Asian city.

The imperial cult, the worship of the spirit of Rome and of the emperor, with its loyalty test of formal incense burnt at the foot of Caesar's statue, found a centre, appropriately enough, in Pergamum, and coloured the city's life. The first temple of the cult was located there in 29 B.C., and is shown as a device on coins down to the principate of Trajan at the end of the first century. In Trajan's honour a second temple was built, and a third was dedicated to Severus. Only the first temple functioned when John wrote his letter from Patmos, but its presence and its ritual was enough to make Rome's authority oppressively apparent in the city. When John's imagery speaks of 'One who holds the sharp two-edged sword', he writes in reference to the imperial power which challenged Christ so strongly in this cathedral centre of the State religion.

The implied hostility to Rome shows how far the clash of Church and State had gone. It is a far cry to Paul who, a generation before, had hoped that the Empire might receive Christ, and find in Christianity the social and political cement which shrewd imperial authority had sought since Augustus' day, to bind into unity the states and cities of the Mediterranean world. The Christians of Pergamum lived in the presence of the dire alternative, for Rome had made her choice, and the Christian religion had been officially proscribed for twenty years. They dwelt, says John, those who followed the faith in Pergamum, 'where Satan's seat is'.

The significance of that phrase has become strikingly apparent since archaeology opened up a more detailed knowledge of the life of Pergamum and the structure of its pagan cults. Paganism lay in three strata. There was an Anatolian substratum represented by the worship of Dionysus, the god of vegetation, and Asklepios, the god of healing. Snakes, and the handling of reptiles, were associated, as a drama of Euripides shows, with the cult of Dionysus. Snakes were the symbol of Asklepios. A Pergamenian coin shows the emperor Caracalla standing spear in hand before a great serpent twined round a bending sapling. He raises his right hand in the salute which Hitler's Nazis brought back to another pagan world. Pausanias, too, the Greek traveller, who has left descriptions of his journeys in the Mediterranean lands, describes the same god enthroned with a staff in his hand and the other hand on the head of a serpent. Christians who associated the serpent with Satan must have found the cult of the god of healing, and his serpent-infested temple, peculiarly revolting and diabolical.

There is no doubt that Pergamum was obsessed with the symbol of the serpent. It was even present in the second stratum which represents a second historical layer in the city's history. Zeus and Athene, worshipped at Pergamum, represent the coming of the Greeks to Asia. Pausanias described the throne-like altar to Zeus on the top of the crag above Pergamum. It was discovered in 1871 and taken to Germany where it stands reconstructed today in the East Berlin Museum, something like a small version of Italy's tasteless Victor Emmanuel monument in Rome. The structure, a perron of steps leading to a great altar, commemorated the defeat of a Gallic invasion two centuries before. The wandering Celts who reached Rome and Delphi in the era of their folk wanderings also infiltrated Asia Minor, where they gave their name to Galatia. Pergamum was strong enough to drive them off and celebrated the deliverance with the altar to Zeus. Its frieze represents the gods of Olympus battling with the giants shown in the sculpture as a brood of muscular warriors with snake-like tails. The Zeus to whom the altar was dedicated was called Zeus the Saviour, another blasphemous offence to Christian minds. Perhaps the altar was actually the 'Satan's seat' of the letter's imagery. . . .

One of the recent curiosities of archaeology was the discovery in the junk-yard of the Worksop Town Council, England, of the battered marble figure of a giant. Experts from the British Museum have pronounced it to be part of the frieze from Pergamum's altar brought to England by the Earl of Arundel, two centuries ago, and fallen on evil days when Worksop Manor was demolished.

The third and topmost stratum represented the Roman period and the imperial cult. Perhaps Antipater, the Antipas of the letter, was the first to suffer martyrdom for rejection of the cult. He died by burning in a brazen bull, says tradition, in Domitian's day, and he must have been one of many in this place of offensive and pervading paganism. Wherever the Christian turned he met the flaunting symbols of the things his whole being rejected, and his mind hated with deep disgust. It helped perhaps to realise that One knew 'where he lived', but for those whose daily lot it was to live in such oppressive proximity to the mingled cults of paganism there was deep temptation to compromise.

The spirit of the city's paganism suggested as much. With astonishing subtlety, Pergamum had mingled and synthetised the deities of three races, of three successive periods in the history of the State. There were pagans, no doubt, who thought that their complex scheme of worship could absorb yet another faith. There were Christians who thought that the notion was not without its merits. Could Christianity avoid a head-on collision with the pagan world, at least with the simple imperial cult, by a little judicious compromise? The thought had its temptation in a place where dissent was more likely to be viewed with hostility and disfavour than anywhere else in Asia. Perhaps Dionysus, Asklepios, Athene, and Zeus could be avoided as objects of worship, impossible though it was to escape their presence in shrine and image. To avoid the worship of the emperor in the centre of his cult, where that worship was thought to conflict with no other, and to be withal a test of true loyalty, was not so easy.

Hence the popularity of the sect of the Nicolaitans in Pergamum. Little is known about them, but it is clear enough that they were those who thought that a measure of compromise could be worked out, perhaps only in the comparatively harmless sphere of the state cult. The apostles saw with devastating clarity that no compromise at all was possible. Allow the pinch of incense before the emperor and the landslide would begin. The guild-feasts would follow, a problem for Christians in Thyatira. Then would come the immoralities of Corinth's worship of Aphrodite, and the breakdown of Christian morality, the sanctities of Christian marriage, the whole challenging distinctiveness of the Christian faith, the whole purpose of its being.

Those who stood firm, in spite of misunderstanding, misrepresentation, the harsh criticism of less rigid friends, and the fierce resentment of a corrupt society, held and passed on the integrity of the faith. Nowhere was it more difficult to stand thus lonely and execrated than in Pergamum, where Christianity and Caesarism confronted each other face to face.

Twenty

Thyatira, City of Jezebel

THE longest of the strange letters which were written from Patmos, and the most difficult to understand, was addressed to the congregation of the church of Thyatira, 20 miles south-east of Pergamum. Heresy was abroad in Thyatira, inspired by a woman who earned the writer's scorn, and it is possible to gain an idea of the nature of her faction only through some understanding of the city itself, its character and its pursuits.

Roads often make cities, and it was a valley-highway which gave place and occasion for the Asian town. Like the railway lines of the nineteenth century, the roads of the ancient world followed naturally the easy routes of the valley floors, and Thyatira, lying in a vale between the Hermus and the Caicus rivers, was a node of communications both when Pergamum ruled the western butt of Asia Minor, and in Roman times when the imperial road ran that way.

Settlement there must have been at a place so advantageous from the earliest times, but the city proper was founded by Seleucus I, Alexander's general, who, of all the successors, inherited the greatest segment of the empire which the young conqueror left behind. Seleucus, dynast of Syria and founder of its Greek kingdom, ruled the old lands of Persia from the Hermus Valley to the mountainous marches of India. His frontiers pressed hard on those of Lysimachus, who clung to the Asian coast as far south as Ephesus. In Thyatira, Seleucus settled a body of Alexander's Macedonian veterans to hold a precarious borderland.

Philetaerus, as described in Chapter XIV, revolted in 282 B.C., and established the kingdom of Pergamum. The new realm formed a convenient buffer state between Seleucus and Lysimachus, but a power thus hemmed in between strong neighbours was not likely to remain satisfied with her living space. Thyatira, deliberately sited as a sentinel, was certain to be contested, and for long years the city no doubt changed hands frequently as Pergamenian or Syrian power ebbed or flowed in the valleys to the west of the Asian plateau.

For all the task the city was called upon to face, Thyatira was not an easily defended site. It had no strong acropolis like Sardis and Pergamum to stand firmly in an invader's path. The city lay on a gentle rise open to determined assault, and fitted only for the rôle of outpost, able to check and delay the drive of an invading army while defence in depth was organised behind. Such a function can be maintained only by determined defenders, ready to make good the lack of natural defence by uncommon valour and vigour of hand. A soldierly spirit was necessary for such a people, and the original Macedonian garrison provided it in full measure. They were men who had marched with Alexander to the Punjab plains, and had known the stern discipline of the Macedonian phalanx.

The old religion of the city reflected its military character. Like the Roman legionaries in Britain, the Macedonian settlers accepted the worship of some local Anatolian patron-hero or god, and he appears on early coins as a warrior figure with a battle-axe on his shoulder. Hence the designation of the triumphant Christ in the letter: 'One whose eyes are like a flame of fire and whose feet are like to fine brass'.

Rome came to Asia with Antiochus' defeat in 189 B.C., and the bequest of Pergamum in 133 B.C. The formation of the province brought peace, and when the days of Republican degeneracy and exploitation were succeeded by the strong rule and organisation of the Empire, prosperity was added to peace. In the last years of Claudius, half-way through the century, Thyatira began to issue its own coinage again, for the first time, as far as the evidence goes, for two full centuries. The coins became progressively more numerous, and in the third century their abundance speaks of a great commercial city. A business woman of Thyatira has been encountered in Philippi selling purple cloth, one of the city's manufactures. The purple or crimson material in which Lydia dealt, was made from the local madder-root, a cheap and effective substitute for the expensive product of the murex shell found chiefly on the Phoenician coast.

The language of Luke in the account suggests that Lydia was a proselyte of the synagogue, and the fact may indicate that the Jews had found Thyatira a convenient centre for commercial activity when trade succeeded war as the city's function. Indeed, the geographical position which had prompted the location of a garrison there, also facilitated the movement of commerce, and ensured that Thyatira should become, under the Roman Peace, a centre of manufacture and exchange. Garments, dyed locally, were a speciality. So were armour and bronze. A coin of Thyatira shows Hephaestus, the divine smith, hammering a helmet on an anvil, and the word in the letter for 'fine brass', 'chalcolibanos', found nowhere else in Greek, may have been a Thyatiran trade name, caught up for local colour by the writer on Patmos.

Commerce, indeed, may have been the crux of the Christians' problem in the city. Inscriptions are not numerous, but they mention workers in wool, linen, leather, and bronze, potters, bakers, dyers, and slavers. Each had their guild like that of the silversmiths of Ephesus. Paul's letter to Corinth is clear indication that the trade-guilds, with their demanding social life, their pagan ritual, and their periodic feasts, were to be a serious problem for the Christian member pledged by conscience to abjure the licentiousness of the world about them. Peter and Jude, whose obscure but biting words castigate the feasts of paganism in which the more liberally minded of their people were taking a damaging and compromising part, are evidence enough of the spiritual danger which the Christians faced. The issue was simply this: were the Christians to withdraw and be separate, or were they temperately to associate with the group-activities of paganism?

To abstain meant misunderstanding, and the unjust charge of churlishness and self-righteous exclusiveness. It meant persecution, and often, for a guild-member dependent upon good-will for his trade, the loss of livelihood and daily bread. To conform meant exposure to the temptations which the Christian had no right to court, to the pervading carnality into which ancient paganism so readily degenerated, and from which the convert had been so hardly redeemed, and to a perilous compromise which left his faith with no distinctive marks, no firm and lofty standards. John, Peter, and Jude saw that there was no real Christian alternative to the harder choice, the more demanding course.

The mysterious woman in the Thyatiran church thought otherwise. 'I hold it against you', says the letter, 'that you suffer the woman Jezebel who calls herself a prophetess, and who seduces my servants to commit fornication and eat things sacrificed to idols'. 'Idol-meat' was the old Corinthian problem. Should a Christian eat meat which came to the butchers' shops from the temple altars?

Paul's answer had been simple. The pagan deity had no reality, and meat was meat, but he added, with a word of stern caution: if a non-Christian made an issue of the practice, or if a puzzled convert was led astray in the process, it would be 'better to abstain from meat all the days of one's life'. It would seem that the matter was increasingly thus made an issue for Christians. It could have been especially a challenge in the guild-feasts of the Thyatiran tradesmen. At the same social functions the dancing slave-girls could have given weight and meaning to the other phrase in the writer's reproach.

Lydia could have been the founder of the Thyatiran church, and could have established in the process a tradition of female leadership. Taking advantage of it, the woman Jezebel 'called herself a prophetess', and taught the church to compromise. The nickname offers another clue to those who seek to understand the letter, and gain some glimpse of the Christian group in Thyatira. In the Old Testament story, Jezebel was the dynamic princess of Tyre. She was married to Ahab of Israel to establish and cement the trade partnership between Samaria and Tyre. The commercial prosperity which followed corrupted the land. Israel provided primary produce. Phoenicia paid for her imports with the luxury goods of her seaborne trade. Ahab was rich. So was his court. But with Phoenician trade and alliance, and with the princess whose marriage promoted both, came the deities of the coast with their licentious worship and deep corruption.

If a woman of Thyatira was teaching Christians to set comfort, conformity, the retention of prosperity, and easy social relationships, first in importance, and to risk the integrity of the faith in the interests of the good things of life, she might very appropriately be called Jezebel, and those familiar with the Old Testament would readily see the point of the apt reproach. Jezebel was no doubt a clever woman with a gift of speech. Anxious Christians, faced with the difficulties of social intercourse which their testimony occasioned, and the peril to their daily livelihood which the hostility of the guild would inevitably produce, were likely to listen to a voice which offered a solution. 'See,' the most obscure verse in the letter runs, 'I am placing her on a dining-couch, and her base associates with her, and they shall enjoy great tribulation, unless they repent. That *she* cannot repent she has demonstrated'. A Thyatiran inscription quoted by Ramsay, shows that it was not customary for respectable women to feast publicly with men. A leading citizen is recorded to have given a religious feast. Men and women were segregated for the occasion. The verse of grim menace probably means that such looseness can only lead to ruin. Therefore let the woman's victims desert her, and leave her to the doom her wilful perversion must inevitably bring. It is a curious threat, and a difficult situation to envisage but, as the old saying has it, the worst is the corruption of the best, and Christianity has known, indeed, still knows, some horrifying perversions.

Meanwhile, the writer concludes, let such malpractices and heretical falsehoods not disguise themselves as deep teaching. She who claimed the name of prophetess no doubt talked of insight into the profounder meaning of the faith, of mystic significance eluding the simpler understanding, of a dichotomy, perhaps of body and soul, which left the pure spirit unsullied in the body's casual shame. Such pernicious nonsense was certainly abroad in the Church a few years later, as the first of John's epistles testifies. Perhaps Thyatira saw the beginnings. 'And so I say to you', the exhortation concludes, 'the rest of those in Thyatira who hold not this teaching, and who have not known 'the deep things' as they call them (the 'deep things of Satan', say I) I put upon you no other burden, but what you have, hold until I come'.

It is a sad picture, half-glimpsed through the poetic words. The story of the early Church is not all one of triumph, endurance, and uprightness. There was division within, as well as hostility without. Those who stood firm in Thyatira in the old martial spirit of their town, were holding a frontier. They held it well.

Twenty-One

Sardis, The City that Died

SARDIS, ancient capital of Lydia, is the most elusive of the cities of Saint John. So completely did it pass from later history. Nothing remains today to indicate past greatness, save some ruins on and under the vast acropolis above the Hermus valley, and the name of a small village on the site, called Sart.

Sardis lay on the junction of the roads from Ephesus, Smyrna, Pergamum and inner Asia Minor. Lydia itself, of which Sardis was the royal seat, lay astride and along two highways from the coast to the highlands of the centre of Asia Minor, and was rich in consequence and a meeting place of culture. In Sardis, Greek and Oriental mingled their civilisation, their enterprise and art.

Before Hellenistic days, and the coming of Alexander's brief empire and its successor kingdom, Sardis was the political centre of Asia Minor. Under Croesus, famed for his vast wealth, Sardis was a proverb for luxury and prosperity. Gold and silver were first struck into coins there, and gold was plentiful in the alluvial silt of the Pactolus which flowed nearby.

But wealth would have been in Sardis with no glitter of gold in the washed river-sand. A site so strategic was marked down by geography for greatness. The broad ridge of Mount Tmolus, famous in ancient story, thrusts seaward from the Anatolian plateau. Under the range are a series of alluvial foothills, and the tooling of nature has made a geological feature of long ridges with steep sides, each terminating northward in a sharp point dominating the valley floor and the Hermus plain, and joined on the south by a narrow neck of land to the mass of Mount Tmolus. On one of these almost impregnable lookouts stood Sardis. In days of peace, under the shadow of Rome, the city overflowed its acropolis and spread prosperously on the plain below, but all through the days when her history was made, Sardis perched on her platform, fifteen hundred feet high, seemingly secure from all the wickedness of men. No doubt farmstead and villa were always found on the valley floor, but the great acropolis was Sardis, the ready refuge in war, and like Troy, the place of royal residence.

Such a position was certainly occupied from the beginnings of time. The stronghold would not miss the canny eyes of the first comers to the river valley, and Sardis must have been an important centre before the Lydian kingdom came into being about 1,200 B.C. 'It was the princely capital,' writes Sir William Ramsay, 'from the time that there began to be princes in Lydia. Nature has made it the overseer of the Hermus Valley, and its foundation marked out its master for the headship first of that valley, and thereafter of the rest of Lydia, whose fate was dependent on the Hermus Valley.'

All history, in fact, speaks of the strategic importance of the place. The Ionian Greeks, in revolt against Persia in 499 B.C., took Sardis and burned it, and in far Susa, at the heart of the great empire, Darius reacted to the loss of a place so sensitive in his remote defences, and set his armies moving. And Darius' son, Xerxes, staging the vast assault on Europe which arose in sequence from the Ionian revolt, assembled at Sardis an armed host which became a legend and an astonishment for its might and numbers as well as for the catastrophe which fell on it.

But that was half a century after the golden age of Croesus, the last of the Lydian kings, whose wealth became a story in Greece and the Middle East. Croesus found lasting fame from the narrative of the best of all story-tellers, the historian Herodotus. Under Croesus the Lydian kingdom reached its peak. He subdued the restless Greeks of the coastal cities, Ephesus, Smyrna, and the rest. He grew arrogant with power, and thus found his way into the pages of the Greek historian, whose philosophy of history was that wealth breeds insolence, and insolence begets ruin, a doctrine not remote from Old Testament thought. Jeshurun grows fat and kicks. Croesus was certainly an illustration.

Persia, in the middle of the sixth century before Christ, was rising mightily in the east, and Croesus could not but mark the fact. 'Croesus,' says Herodotus, 'learned that Cyrus had destroyed the empire of Astyages, and that the Persians were becoming daily more powerful. This led him to consider with himself whether it were possible to check the growing power of that people before it came to a head.' What happened next was the story the Greeks loved to tell. Croesus knew and admired the Greeks. Solon, the Athenian lawgiver, had once visited him in Sardis, and warned him to beware of self-satisfaction, and to count no man as happy, until the end of life had set him free at last from all danger of a sudden change of fortune. Said Solon: 'Sire, he who unites the greatest number of advantages, and, retaining them to the day of his death, then dies in peace, that man alone is, in my judgment, entitled to bear the name of "happy". In every matter it behoves us to mark well the end, for often God gives men a gleam of happiness, and then plunges them into ruin'.

Perhaps that was why, in preparing his war, Croesus took every possible precaution. He tested out, by ingenious devices, the various oracles of the Greek world, and found that the oracle of Delphi was thoroughly reliable. This oracle, therefore, he consulted. Should he go to war? Apollo's reply was: 'If you cross the River Halys you will destroy a great empire.' He crossed the Halys, met the Persians in battle, and destroyed a great empire—his own.

Croesus retired to his mountain fortress with his shattered army, determined to retrieve his fortunes in the following year, but he had reckoned without the military genius of the Persians' new leader. Cyrus had the king shut up in Sardis before he could mobilise his second army. Confident in the natural strength of his city, Croesus prepared to sit the invaders out. Herodotus may take up the story: 'On the fourteenth day of the siege, Cyrus made proclamation that he would give a reward to the man who should first mount the wall. After this he made an assault but without success. His troops retired, but one Hyroeades, resolved to approach the citadel and attempt it at a place where no guards were ever set. On this side the rock was so precipitous, and the citadel so impregnable, that no fear was entertained of its being carried in this place . . . Hyroeades, however, had observed a Lydian soldier descend the rock to retrieve a helmet which had rolled down from the top, and having seen the man pick it up and carry it back, thought over what he had witnessed, and formed his plan. He climbed the rock himself, and other Persians followed in his track, until a large number had mounted to the top. Thus Sardis was taken.'

It was all due to the fact, said the Greeks, that Meles of old had not carried the sacred lion round the ramparts at this point. Meles was the founder of Sardis, and had it in his power by heaven's gift to make his city impregnable by this ritual. He had looked at the sheer cliff, and thought it unnecessary tp perform the rite at this point. Such tragic flaws are part of an ancient universal conviction, embedded in many a myth, from Achilles' heel to Baldur's mistletoe . . .

There is always a thing forgotten
When all the world goes well . . .

So came disaster to Sardis.

In fact, the fault lay with geology. The ridge of Sardis was built of crumbling rock. The great cliffs appeared mighty, but literally had feet of clay, mud lightly compacted, and continually eroded by wind, rain, and frost. Little, indeed, now remains of the plateau where the city stood, and the road which traversed the connecting neck of land. Twenty or more centuries have worn it away. Meles may have laid his fortifications with care and precision, and carried his totem right round, but the slow wear of seven hundred winters had built funnels and clefts which determined men could scale.

Carelessness and over-confidence born of apparent strength brought a disaster which rang through the world. 'Solon, Solon!' sighed Croesus when he was led to the stake. Cyrus stayed the execution and asked him what he meant. The broken king told of the Athenian's visit, and his warning, and in a burst of pity the conqueror spared him to become a symbol of the precarious prosperity of men, and a text for the moralizing of the Greeks.

After Alexander, Sardis became a city in Antigonus' realm, then passed into the control of the Seleucids of Syria, and finally into the possession of Pergamum, when the family of Attalus carved out their kingdom from the western provinces of the Syrian kings. It was during the unstable years in which the Seleucid power ebbed and flowed in those far marches of empire that history curiously repeated itself. Cyrus had taken Sardis in 549 B.C. In 214 B.C. Sardis was at war with Antiochus the Great. Antiochus shut his enemy up in the stronghold exactly as his Persian predecessor had done, and the city was again captured by the enterprise of a soldier, who found a way up seemingly formidable cliffs. The lesson of past history had not been learned. Past experience had been carelessly forgotten. Men grew slack, and in the moment of need Sardis failed the population which trusted to appearances, and failed to stand on guard.

And yet Sardis was conscious of her history, even in Roman days. She had passed into Rome's hands by the will of Attalus III, last king of Pergamum, who, sensing the winds of change in Asia, had bequeathed his realm to the rising power by the Tiber. The city accepted the fact, and was made one of Asia's official centres. When the cities of Asia contended for the second temple to the Emperor, in A.D. 26, the envoys, as Tacitus tells the story, had long orations to make on the past glory of their city. It is quite certain that those who lived in John's day knew the story, and that they would remember vividly many a fact of history as they read the reproach against a church which had a name for life and was dead. As cities do, Sardis lived on in decay. The great earthquake of A.D. 17 was a fierce blow, and there was little left of history for the ancient fortress save the brief glory of Diocletian's day, when Sardis became a capital of the new province of Lydia.

Such was Sardis. 'It was a city,' says Ramsay, 'whose history conspicuously and pre-eminently blazoned forth the uncertainty of human fortunes, the weakness of human strength and the shortness of the step which separates over-confident might from sudden and irreparable disaster. It was a city whose name was almost synonymous with pretentions unjustified, promise unfilled, appearance without reality, confidence which heralded ruin.'

In the light of the city's history the apocalyptic letter to Sardis is curiously vivid in its imagery. Sardis had too often betrayed her trust and fallen short of expectations. Its church revealed, as Christian communities, for good or ill, do reveal, something of the spirit of the place. It had a name for life, doubtless once justified, but was in truth dead. Its works 'were not fulfilled before God'. The task, that is, like the city's fortifications twice in history, remained incomplete in vital points. Like Sardis it had, nevertheless, received great advantages. Like Sardis it had used them ill, and had now to fear sudden overthrow and extinction. 'I will come upon you,' says the divine Critic, 'like a thief, and you will not know during what hour I shall come.' Note the phrase. It is not 'at what hour'. Such visitations are less nicely placed. Man's duty is to be watchful, not at fixed hours, but over all the length of days. Could any reader of the letter in Sardis hear the phrase, and not remember Hyroeades, or the Cretan mercenary of Antiochus, creeping, climbing in the night, testing footholds on the crumbling stone, crouching as stone and pebble tumbled away in the darkness, but coming higher, nearer, while the sentinels slept and all seemed secure in the careless town? So spiritual death creeps on men. Preoccupied with their own affairs, they do not recognize the deadly nature of the torpor which lays hold on mind and heart until the character is changed.

But there were a few who had not 'defiled their garments'. How the bulk of the Sardian church had offended we do not know. The worship of Cybele was strong in the region. Columns of her temple still stand on the valley floor under the eroded remains of Sardis' acropolis, but of the nature of her worship in Sardis we know nothing. It no doubt conformed to the cult of this goddess whose rites were peculiarly Asiatic and primitive, full of wild excitement, the noise of clashing cymbals, blaring horns, and obscene mutilations. Catullus' awful poem, *Attis*, throws lurid light upon it. Perhaps the Nicolaitan heresy had preached too easy a compromise with the cult of the goddess. The sect is not mentioned by name, but the reference to the defiling of garments is a clear indication of unworthy conduct on the part of members of the Christian community. Clean garments for worship were the rule of all ancient worship, and the culprits in the Sardian church had somehow disqualified themselves for Christian communion. If the analogy of all the other letters holds good, the sphere of temptation to unbecoming conduct would be some form of social paganism. In Sardis that temptation would be connected either with the worship of Cybele, or with the Emperor-cult. The latter must have been strong in Sardis. Tiberius had been a most present help to the people in their day of earthquake disaster, and the eagerness with which the city sought permission to build a temple in his name was indication of its allegiance.

Those who still held true were to walk in white. Their reward was to be continuance in the purity they had held at such a cost, and in such a place. The name of Sardis was to be blotted from history. Their reward was 'in no wise' to be blotted from a Book more permanent. Their triumph was secure. White was the colour of triumph. On days of festival the Roman always wore a white toga, and 'to walk in white' suggested victory, gladness at last, and heavenly festival.

Ramsay adds a curious detail. 'Sardis to-day,' he wrote at the turn of the century, 'is a wilderness of ruins and thorns, pastures and wild flowers, where the only habitations are a few huts of Yuruk nomads beside the temple of Cybele in the low ground by the Pactolus. And yet in a sense a remnant has escaped and still survives, which does not indeed excite the same loving tenderness as makes itself felt in the latter part of this letter, yet assuredly merits our sympathy and interest. In the plain of the Hermus which Sardis once dominated there are a few scattered villages whose inhabitants, though nominally Mohammedans, are clearly marked off by certain customs from the Turkish population around. Their women usually bear Christian names, though the men's names are of the ordinary Mohammedan class; they have a kind of priest who wears a black head-dress, not the white turban of the Mohammedans' imams; the villages hold private assemblies when these "black-heads" pay them visits; they practise strict monogamy, and divorce (which is so easy for true Mohammedans) is not permitted; they drink wine and violate other Mohammedan rules and prohibitions; and it is believed by some persons who have mixed with them that they would become Christians forthwith if it did not mean death to do so.' Are these the remains of the Sardian church?

Such is the sad epilogue. Of the beginnings nothing is known. Probably Sardis was evangelised from Ephesus. An inscription dating from the first century, and recording the burial of one Artemas, a physician, was discovered in 1912. Artemas appears to have been a Christian, for the epitaph closes with the words 'He is living'. It is possible that he knew John in the apostle's old age.

From 1910 to 1914 the American archaeologist H. C. Butler, dug at Sardis. His expedition was the first of the magnificently equipped 'digs' by which America has so richly served the cause of archaeology. Professor Paul MacKendrick describes it: Butler, he says, 'had not only a light railway, but a locomotive, used to haul around the site a twenty ton crane for raising large blocks. The great crane now lies abandoned near the temple, its rusted remains as impressive in their way as the temple itself. The workmen decorated the new engine with evergreens and flowers. Various parts of the site were interconnected by telephone, and the excavation house, Omphale, was palatial . . . ' Under the joint patronage of Harvard and Cornell, excavations are proceeding again in an attempt to discover Croesus' palace.

Results were notable. The temple mentioned above was Sardis' shrine of Artemis, with whom, under the influence of the Ephesus-cult, Cybele was identified. It was a magnificent example of monumental Ionic architecture, measuring 160 by 200 feet, and covering 5,000 square yards. It was begun in Alexander's time, for new coins of that date were found in the base of a statue, but it was never finished for most of the sixty-five foot columns were still unfluted. Two still stand to almost their full height. Thirteen still have half their length intact. There were seventy-eight columns in all. The pedestals of some were still rough, awaiting, presumably, carving like those of Ephesus.

A mortgage deed of approximately 300 B.C. gives a glimpse into the wealth of the temple, and the business which centred there. One Mnesimachus acknowledges 'gold lent on deposit, and belonging to Artemis'. He names whole villages and slaves as security, so the sum must have been considerable.

The temple appears to have been used for Christian purposes, for the cross has been here and there cut into the stone. At the eastern end a brick chapel has been found, its altar a crudely cut block of limestone, set on a short section of a column.

Twenty-Two

Philadelphia the Valiant

PHILADELPHIA, whose name means 'brotherly love' was founded in the middle of the second century before Christ, and named by its founder, Eumenes of Pergamum, in honour of his loyal brother Attalus. The city was a 'little Athens', an outpost of Greek culture in Asia, but had little history until the great earthquake of A.D. 17 brought shocking and notable catastrophe. The disaster is thus described by Tacitus, the Roman historian: 'The same year twelve famous cities of Asia collapsed because of an earthquake which took place at night, a calamity the more serious because it fell without warning. Escape into open country, which is the usual resource in such cases, was no help because people were swallowed up by the gaping earth. Great mountains, it is said, crumbled to rubble, and plains were thrust up into hills, while fires glowed amid the ruins. Sardis suffered most sharply and won most pity . . . ' The story continues with details of Caesar's bounteous earthquake-relief, and lists Philadelphia in the third place among the recipients.

The trouble with Philadelphia, however, was that there was no end to disaster. The city seems to have been nearest to the faultline. It stands at the edge of an old volcanic district, named in ancient times 'the Burntland', from the masses of scoria debris and lava which strew the countryside, and proximity to this area of disturbance seems to have rendered the city for a long time subject to earth tremors of a demoralizing nature. Strabo, the Greek geographer, writing in A.D. 20, said, 'Philadelphia is full of earthquakes . . . its very walls are unreliable, but daily in one way or another heave and fall apart'. Escape to the surrounding countryside was a common experience, and many would live for long periods in tents on the safer ground. Hence the imagery of the apocalyptic letter: 'I will make him a pillar in the temple of my God, and he shall go out thence no more.'

In gratitude to Tiberius for his generous relief the city took a new name. It called itself Neocaesarea, but with the lapse of years the old name reasserted itself. The Philadelphians, in other words, tried unsuccessfully to write upon themselves 'the name of their god'.

The letter from Patmos doubtless refers to this. Curiously enough, in the reign of Vespasian, in the seventies of the first century, Philadelphia again made the attempt and called itself Flavia after the ruler's family. On second and third century coins the name occasionally crops up, but it does not seem to have established itself.

When Eumenes of Pergamum founded Philadelphia he chose a notable situation. South-east from the Hermus Valley, a long vale runs into the main plateau of Asia Minor. Up this vale passes the main line of communication between Smyrna and Lydia, and Phrygia. The Roman post-road in the first century passed through Troas, Pergamum and Sardis to Philadelphia, making that city a stage on the main line of Imperial communication.

Hence the cryptic phrase in John's letter: 'I have set before thee an open door which none can shut'. Philadelphia was the keeper of the gateway to the central regions of Asia Minor, a city conscious of its mission as a centre of Hellenism, and aware of its frontier position. That rôle was to be strikingly illustrated in later centuries when Rome had fallen, and Constantinople, her surviving successor, was facing the pressure of Islam, rolling in from Asia and the East.

Heathendom seems to have been no special problem to the church in Philadelphia. In a vine-growing district the worship of Dionysus with its 'enthusiastic' ritual was probably established, but the problem in Philadelphia was neither Nicolaitanism nor authoritarian persecution. It was the Jewish synagogue, which fought the church with every refinement of opposition.

Smyrna and Philadelphia were alike in this respect. They had a virulent, active Jewish nationalist community who were the chief opponents of Christian witness. Ignatius, in his letter to the same church, speaks of the persecuting activities of the Jews of Philadelphia. And as in the case of Smyrna the title of Jew is denied to those who turned it into a name of nationalism. The true 'Jew' is the true interpreter of divine privilege. Hence the relevance of the Jewish imagery in the opening of the letter. The Jews, so called, were no longer the stewards. Like Shebna they had been set aside, and another kept the oracles. Sentence of excommunication had doubtless been pronounced in the synagogue, with all pomp and ceremony, against those who had seceded, and sensitive souls are not unaffected by such portentous formalities. Let them not fear, says the letter, Another has the key of David, and gives it, not to rejected Jewry, but to His faithful. And no man shall close what they open.

The synagogue has passed away. So, too, have all vestiges of the proud cult of Rome and of the Emperor. No trace remains of the Greek religions of Dionysus and Asklepios which once flourished in the town. The Turk, it is true, has come, and the one-time Greek and Christian town lies behind the high-water mark of the great Moslem tide. Its soil, none the less, is rich with blood honourably shed in battle against the conquerors from the east, and it was only division among the Christians which gave the invading Moslems the victory, a Turkish-Byzantine alliance which finally broke the valiant town. The fact is a sad light on Medieval Christendom. That was at the end of the fourteenth century, but Philadelphia still stands. It is the town of Ala Sheher, the 'Red City', named not from its outpoured lives, but from the volcanic earth around. Early in the present century five Christian churches still housed a considerable community and their bishop. Of the remnant now left, there are no statistics. After the treaty which ended the Turkish war of 1922 an exchange of minorities took place between Turkey and Greece. By this agreement, as Osbert Lancaster has written acidly, 'which was hailed by international planners and liberal intellectuals as a triumph of peaceful collaboration . . . an already overcrowded Greece was landed with one and a half million refugees from homes which they had inhabited since at least as early as the eighth century B.C., and which they had maintained against the Phrygians, the Persians, the Romans, the Goths, the Arabs, and the Turks, only finally being forced to render them up at the command of the League of Nations'.

To Philadelphia's valiant frontier battle with the Turks, Gibbon pays eloquent tribute. His stately passage is found in Chapter 64 of his great *Decline and Fall*, and reads like the roll of a funeral drum. Philadelphia's 'open door' was closed on the alien, and took fearful battering before it fell. Here are Gibbon's words:

'In the loss of Ephesus the Christians deplored the fall of the first angel, the extinction of the first candlestick . . . the desolation is complete; and the temple of Diana and the Church of Mary will equally elude the search of the curious traveller. The circus and three stately theatres of Laodicea are now peopled with wolves and foxes; Sardis is reduced to a miserable village; the God of Mahomet, without rival or a son, is invoked in the mosques of Thyatira and

Pergamum, and the populousness of Smyrna is supported by the foreign trade of the Turks and Armenians. Philadelphia alone has been saved by prophecy or courage. At a distance from the sea, forgotten by the emperors, encompassed on all sides by the Turks, her valiant citizens defended their religion and freedom above four-score years, and at length capitulated with the proudest of the Ottomans. Among the Greek colonies and churches of Asia, Philadelphia is still erect—a column in a scene of ruins—a pleasing example that the paths of honour and safety may sometimes be the same.'

Twenty-Three

Laodicea, The City of Wealth

IN a broad valley system on the borders of Phrygia, lay three cities of the New Testament, Colossae, Hierapolis, and Laodicea. The church of Laodicea received the sternest of the letters of John. Colossae was the scene of strange heresies which provoked a letter of Paul. Hierapolis has brief mention in the apostle's closing verses. Philemon, whose slave Onesimus was befriended by Paul in Rome, was a Christian of Colossae. Archippus, his son, was in all probability the leader of the Laodicean Church. The three communities were intimately bound together, and lay only a few miles apart. Hierapolis, of which extensive ruins, including those of a Christian church, remain, was near the source of Laodicea's water-supply. The 'gate of Phrygia', as it was anciently called, lies in the valley-complex, and the area is thermal. There are hot springs on the Maeander at Hierapolis, and warm mud-baths on its banks.

Laodicea stood where the Lycus valley joined the Maeander, like Thyatira, the guardian of the road. Significantly, the western ingress was called the 'Ephesian Gate'. The traveller left the city on the east by the 'Syrian Gate', for the great road ran to Antioch where other roads branched, to the Euphrates valley, to Damascus, and to the north-east, where the desert trade-routes ran towards the great mountains, the Gobi, and the remote lands of the unknown East. The Mongol had not yet sundered Europe and Asia, East and West.

Like Thyatira, Laodicea was no natural fortress. The low eminence, on which its Seleucid fortifications stood, might have presented a difficult problem for an invader, but as a strong-point Laodicea had a serious weakness. The water-supply came principally by a vulnerable aqueduct from springs six miles away to the north in the direction of Hierapolis. A place with its water so exposed to enemy action could scarcely stand a determined siege. The conduit was buried but was not a secret which could be kept.

With the Roman Peace, Laodicea lost all of her frontier character.

Roads serve peace as well as war, and under Rome Laodicea grew in commercial importance. Cicero travelled that way in 51 B.C. on his way to the provincial governorship of Cilicia, and the fact that he cashed drafts in Laodicea shows that the city was already a place of financial importance and considerable wealth. There were manufactures too. The valley produced a glossy black wool, and the strain of sheep bred for the trade was to be traced in the area until the nineteenth century. The wool was the basis of a textile industry centred both in Colossae and in Laodicea. It competed with the products of the Gallic Nervii.

Laodicea had a medical school. The names of its physicians appear on coins as early as the principate of Augustus, and there is also the device of the serpent-wreathed rod of Asklepios, the god of healing. It was probably the medical school of Laodicea which developed the Phrygian eye-powder, famous in the ancient world. It is a fair guess that it was the dried mud of the thermal springs. Emulsified, and heavily impregnated with mineral oils and chemicals, such mud would dry into a fine grey powder, which would conveniently mix with pure water to form a kaolin poultice, an effective remedy for inflammation.

It will be readily seen how these marks and features of the valley-city provided the pattern for the scornful imagery of the apocalyptic letter. 'Because you say: "I am rich, I have grown wealthy, I need nothing", and do not realise that you are wretched, and pitiable, and poor, and blind, and naked, I counsel you to buy of me gold tried in the fire that you may become rich, and to put on white garments that the shame of your nakedness may not appear, and smear salve upon your eyes that you may see'. The black garments exported all over the Mediterranean world, the famous eye ointment, the city's wealth, all are there, forming a structure for the writer's reproaches, with a sting for Laodiceans.

It is possible that the letter quoted the very words of some civic inscription. In A.D. 60 a terrible earthquake, of the sort to which Asia Minor has been perennially subject, 'prostrated the city'. The phrase is that of the historian Tacitus, who wrote of it fifty years later. The Roman Senate at the time gave vast sums to devastated Asian cities in earthquake relief, but the historian records with surprise that Laodicea refused all such aid. She rose again, writes Tacitus, 'with no help from us'. The proud fact would undoubtedly be recorded on stone, and would make a theme for orators. Perhaps

Jewish bankers aided such finance. Two years after the earthquake, in A.D. 62, the governor of Asia refused to allow the annual contribution, made by the local Jews to the temple funds in Jerusalem, to leave the country. It was twenty pounds weight in gold. This sum, a collection set aside by one section of the community alone, and for one special purpose, is a vivid light on the city's wealth.

In prosperity men too commonly decay, and the Christian community of the city had become infected with the spirit of the place. If Archippus of Colossae ministered there, a gentle hint in Paul's letter may thus find explanation. 'Take heed to the ministry you have received that you fulfil it', the warning ran. That was almost a generation before John wrote his scornful words, and the church over that period had lost all fervour and passion. The city on the great, open high-road may have learned the arts of pliancy and compromise in the school of history, and now she was 'neither cold nor hot'. So, too, was the church which found a place in the same self-confident, easy-going community. 'So', the warning continues, 'because you are lukewarm, and neither hot nor cold, I am going to spit you out of my mouth.' The sharp crudity of the phrase must have shocked the audience, but it is more than likely that local colour again provided the vivid imagery. In any thermal area waters of cold streams mingle with the hot chemical-impregnated effluents of thermal springs. The result is a lukewarm mixture, nauseating in the extreme. In the gardens of Te Aroha, or at a spring near Lake Rotoma in New Zealand, such warm soda-laden waters may be tasted with the immediate temptation to do as the writer to Laodicea threatens he will do. The sickly mixture, neither refreshingly cold, nor beneficently hot, and burdened with alien content, disgusts. So did Laodicea disgust its bishop, and the One in whose name he wrote.

Perhaps the Christians of Laodicea had bought peace by compromise. The sharp edge was gone from their doctrine, and lukewarmness of testimony avoided all offence by avoiding distinctiveness and challenge. In such fashion authority was reconciled, and a clash with the synagogue averted. A synagogue there must certainly have been, although the epistle mentions no word about the Jews. The amount of the confiscated temple-tax implies a population of 7,500 adult Jewish freemen, not counting women and children. Twenty or more years later the figure could hardly have been less. At neighbouring Hierapolis the Jews left many marks behind in surviving inscriptions. There is a record of the trade-guilds into which they were organised, purple-dyers, for example, and carpet-makers. Certain special rights enjoyed by the Jewish community are also recorded. In Laodicea they can hardly have been less active.

Whatever the cause, ease, wealth, prosperity, the pervading spirit of the place, the life of the church-community was at a low ebb in Laodicea. It is curious that such a state should accompany an absence of enemies or persecution. Whether cause or effect is to be seen in such a situation cannot be known. Perhaps it provides an illustration of Toynbee's doctrine of Challenge and Response. Opulence and a facile environment have not been normally the stimuli of human progress. The pressure of hard and difficult conditions has been rather the prerequisite of achievement. Physically at ease, Laodiceans of every age, and of all varieties, have grown indifferent to the call to work and strive for excellence.

At the head of the Laodicean letter stands a Figure girt with authority. He is the 'Amen', who underlines with stern verity the threat and promise which lies in the letter, and which looming test and persecution were to bring to historical reality. He also calls Himself 'the faithful and true witness', and the words launch a shaft at the task and duty of testimony which a self-satisfied group had sadly neglected. Finally, He is 'the beginning of the creation of God'. Those words were read in the congregation's hearing in the mid-eighties of the century. Older members of the audience would be sharply reminded of another letter, over another great signature, which was heard first in the same place over twenty years before. The letter of Paul to the Colossians was, by the writer's direction, read also in the church at Laodicea, and in its first chapter was Paul's magnificent and historic exaltation of Christ. No Laodicean could fail to see the link between the two communications, see the point of the reminder, and realise that it was Majesty all-divine which called them back to zeal and dedication in the words from Patmos.

So closes the letter, the century, and the list of the cities of the New Testament. Years of obscurity follow. The State's mad policy of persecution was to cast shadows on the path. The canon of scripture was complete. Great men appear and pass, but in comparison with the first century the second is poor in documents, and obscure in much of its history. The Church at large emerged from its trials and testings coherent, strong, and undefeated. The triumph was due to the foundations widely and well laid in the century of Christ and

His apostles. It is thanks to their labours, and the endurance of their converts, thanks to their zeal, frankness, penetrating understanding, and selfless toil that the Church endured and survived. In the cities of the New Testament lies the record and memorial, their labour and their varied enterprise.